BIRDS

BIRDS

The Goldfinch, Birds, Art and Us

Simon Schama
Martine Gosselink

Mauritshuis | HANNIBAL

FOREWORD
Why *BIRDS*? p. 8
Martine Gosselink

INTRODUCTION
Oh, for the Wings... p. 14
Simon Schama

Who Doesn't Want to be Friends with *The Goldfinch*? p. 46
Adrienne Quarles van Ufford

Bird Artists p. 156
Eva Meijer

Birds of a Feather p. 160
Laura Cumming

What If All the Birds Fell Out of the Sky? p. 166
Philip Hoare

Carpaccio and Birds p. 172
Stefan Hertmans

Birds in World Literature p. 177

Bibliography p. 196

Photo Credits p. 199

Colophon p. 200

BIRDS through the eyes of Martine Gosselink

Stilled Flight

p. 56

The Fate of the Flightless

p. 74

Plumage

p. 86

Envying Avians

p. 104

The Genius of Birds

p. 112

Heavenly Messengers

p. 122

Lovebirds

p. 142

Why *BIRDS*?

Martine Gosselink

On 13 May 2023, I read the following headline in *The Guardian*: 'Simon Schama on the broken relationship between humans and nature: "The joke's on us. Things are amiss."' It introduced an extract from the opening chapter of *Foreign Bodies*, the latest book by the acclaimed British writer, (art) historian and TV presenter. Two things struck me about the piece. As always with Schama's writing, the erudition and eloquence were admirable. But, despite my not entirely inadequate knowledge in the area under discussion, I was shocked by the alarming message. I could have cried.

I read: 'A south Asian vulture population of 40 million in the 1980s now numbers around 19,000 forty years later. This is more than a catastrophic species loss, bad enough though that is. The dramatic depletion of vultures has unpicked the ecological threads that have tied human and animal culture together in India for centuries. The reverent freedom given to sacred cows by Hinduism, so that they might wander the streets until their bodies lie down in peaceful death, depended on the working assumption that carcasses would be cleaned by scavenging vulture flocks. Without the vultures, decomposing cattle have attracted rats and feral dogs, whose numbers have increased exponentially as the birds have disappeared. A collateral result is the steeply rising incidence of rabid attacks on humans, many of them fatal.'

Here is another extract: 'This shrinking of distance between wild and human habitats has also encouraged the long-distance traffic in wild animals. In 2005, it was estimated that each year of the previous decade had seen the live trafficking of 40,000 primates, 640,000 reptiles, 4 million birds and 350 million fish, numbers that have almost certainly increased in the years since.'

In this way, Schama points out many abuses. All these examples are a source of profound sadness. The relationship between humans and animals is completely out of balance. And humans themselves will ultimately suffer. Pandemics and climate crises will be rampant. Simon Schama tells it the way it is, sparing no one, certainly not those responsible.

The *Guardian* article prompted the Mauritshuis to ask Schama to act as guest curator for the exhibition *BIRDS*, which focuses on the relationship between humans and birds. *The Goldfinch* (1654) – for decades one of the most beloved paintings in the museum – is not only an extraordinarily endearing finch portrayed by the seventeenth-century painter Carel Fabritius. As a bird species, the finch has been important to humans for centuries. Humans taught this bird to draw water from a container using a thimble-sized bucket, hence its nickname in Dutch: *putter* or *puttertje* (little *putter*). The word *putten* means to draw water, therefore a *putter* or *puttertje* refers to the person (or animal) that draws water. Humans have also attributed a religious significance to the bird. We will return to this in more detail later.

I contacted Simon and he immediately said yes. I jumped for joy! Now, two years later, the time has come: everything is ready and our dreams have come true. Throughout this preparatory period, we sent each other messages – from London, New York, Amsterdam and elsewhere – about birds we encountered along the way, whether on a balcony, in a park, a museum or in nature, or the traces they left, for instance as droppings on a windowsill. We laughed about those strange birds and ourselves, and I learned a lot from Simon. It has been a great privilege to have been able to spar and play with this knowledgeable, wise, funny and empathetic man. I have cherished every minute of our collaboration.

Simon Schama and *The Goldfinch* invited winged creatures from all corners of the world to take part in the exhibition: birds that have all been involved by humankind in the human world, sometimes with the complicity of the birds themselves, but often in an imposed relationship.

As we set about planning this book and exhibition, we were constantly confronted with the vast scope of the theme, the relationship between humans and birds. Because we focused primarily on this relationship, we dropped almost all topics relating solely to the life of birds themselves. But even so... Birds have been flying and walking on the Earth for 150 million years. There are 11,000 species of birds, 500 of which have been observed in the Netherlands alone. These species all fall under the term 'bird', but many are as different from one another as night and day. We have interacted with many of these distinct bird species for as long as humanity has existed. Every culture has its own way of dealing with the species in its environment, and has its own history in that regard. As a result, countless meanings have been attributed to birds throughout the ages, in legends, fairy tales, stories, religions, poems, musical compositions and artistic works. Where to start our story was therefore a difficult question – but where to stop even more so.

To give you an idea, we will embark on a short journey through folklore and legends about mythical birds. In Denmark, the supernatural raven Valravn, who was once a knight, can only break the curse by drinking the blood of a boy. In the Indian state of Manipur, the story is told of Hayainu, a girl who turns herself into a hornbill to escape her cruel stepmother. Herodotus, Aristotle, Pliny and Aelian all mention the crocodile bird, which enjoys a symbiotic relationship with the Nile crocodile, whose throat and teeth it keeps clean. A martlet in English heraldry is a bird without feet that never roosts, from birth to death. Lui-kong-tsiau is the name of a bird in Taiwan: the sky darkens as soon as it perches in the treetops and the storm will break as soon as it crows. In the Philippines, the limokon is considered an omen bird; it helps people with trade and communicates with the dead. For the Sumerians, King Etana ascended to heaven with the help of an eagle. The Romans had caladrius, a white bird that healed the sick by taking over their ailments. The Chinese guhuoniao bird abducts infants and then raises them itself. In 570, the year of Muhammad's birth, the ababil birds protected the holy Kaaba in Mecca from the army of the Ethiopian ruler Abraha by dropping stones on the latter's elephants. Aceh in northern Sumatra is home to Si Parkit Raja Parakeet, 'the king of parakeets', who escaped from a golden cage. And in large parts of Asia, the kalaviṅka is worshipped as an immortal bird with a human head who sang while still in its egg and who preaches the teachings of Buddha.

There is no end to these avian stories. Nor to many other subjects to do with the relationship between humans and birds. Nevertheless, we sought to outline a framework. An obvious subject would have been birds in art – after all, millions of birds have been depicted in the visual arts over the centuries – but we did not take this as our starting point. So what did we turn our attention to?

Well, hunting, for example, in the chapter entitled *Stilled Flight*. We hunt birds to eat them or put them in cages, but we also use birds to hunt: hawks and peregrine falcons are trained to catch rabbits, hares and ducks. *The Fate of the Flightless* focuses on birds as a source of food. We eat not only the meat of chickens, ducks, geese, quails and pigeons, but also their eggs. In some countries, it is customary to eat birds' nests.

We admire birds for their colourful plumage, which we were only too happy to acquire for ourselves to ornament our hats and boas. Feathers are the focus of the chapter called *Plumage*.

Birds are special on account of their song, their dance, their colours, but above all because they can do something we can't, which is to fly. You can read more about this in *Envying Avians*. The flying ability of birds has led humans to study them and make use of their specific characteristics in our aviation technology. Researchers are also interested in the aerodynamics and navigation capacity of birds. You can read more about this in *The Genius of Birds*.

In countless cultures and religions, birds act as mystical mediators between heaven and earth. This is the focus of *Heavenly Messengers*. In the seventeenth century, virtually everyone understood the lesson to be learned from a painting showing a girl next to an empty birdcage: she was no longer a virgin. Learn more about the sexual connotations and romantic meanings we have projected on to birds in the chapter entitled *Lovebirds*.

However, these perspectives paint anything but a complete picture of the numerous relationships that exist between humans and birds. For example, this book doesn't cover genetic research on chicken embryos, or the question of how birdsong is influenced by human sounds. You will learn nothing about how geese were trained as guard animals, about their relationship with the Roman goddess Juno, or about the fact that their fat was used to treat wounds. And you can forget about the fairy tales of Mother Goose; the board game called The Game of the Goose and its history; or the fact that geese were considered a type of fish, which means that Christians were allowed to eat them during Lent.[1] Nor will we look into the role of birds in heraldry and vexillology (that is, the study of flags). Regardless of how special the stork has been, and still is, as a centuries-old symbol for the Hague, we will not delve into it, nor will we explore bird behaviour, which has been studied since time immemorial to predict the weather. But other elements, both familiar and surprising, will be examined. Read on in the knowledge that there are vast textual and visual riches to be found between heaven and earth about our bond with our winged friends.

There is, we know, a great deal of despair in the world about the state of biodiversity in general and about the decline in birdlife on the planet, in particular the decline caused by humans. But there is also hope. In the course of this project, all those involved couldn't help but talk to others about birds. It was remarkable how we all became contaminated by a positive variant of 'bird flu', as it were, and how many responses this triggered. People looked at birds with new eyes, and interest in avifauna grew week by week. People reached out to us with all sorts of things, from sound recordings captured in a forest to bird apps that allow you to identify species by their song. We received tips about birds in art, music and literature, as well as about how to interact with birds in your garden or on your balcony. One afternoon, just as I was starting to write a paragraph about birds and love, two white doves landed in my garden. I had never seen them there before. Once I had finished the passage, they flew off. I was left with the feeling that we had worked together briefly, the doves and I. That same afternoon, Simon messaged me from his home in New York State: 'Amazing – as I was writing birdy stuff, a hummingbird (sacred to the Maya and Aztecs!) flew into our glass-walled living room, got frantic, kept flying into an abstract triptych by David Rankin, a friend of ours. It took me nearly 20 minutes of arm-flapping Big Birdyness for the sweet tiny thing to find an exit! I think word has got round about our exhibition in the avian world!' This is no doubt wishful thinking on the part of two people who were deeply immersed in their bird bubble, but who are also convinced that humans and birds are inextricably linked and that we must continue to make this bond visible. Who knows, perhaps the beauty of all the pieces featured in this book and exhibition will lead to a growing interest in birds.

Together Simon and I assembled an anthology of writings about humans and birds. This means that, in addition to the topics mentioned above, we have included a separate section that collects excerpts from fairy tales, fables, stories and poems, from ancient times to the present day, from China to Suriname and everywhere in between.

In addition to the essays by Simon Schama, Adrienne Quarles van Ufford and myself, we asked a number of writers to contribute to this book. Simon approached the British authors Laura Cumming and Philip Hoare: Laura on account of her award-winning book *Thunderclap: A Memoir of Art & Life & Sudden Death* (2023) about *The Goldfinch*, Carel Fabritius and other Dutch painters; Philip, not only on account of his inventive books starring whales and other inhabitants of the sea, but of course also for his book *Albert & the Whale* (2021), in which he explains that Albrecht Dürer would forever change our view of nature through art. The idea to involve writer-philosopher Eva Meijer, the author of *Bird Cottage* (2018), was a priceless tip from Tommy Wieringa. Approaching Flemish writer Stefan Hertmans was the joint brainwave of publisher Gautier Platteau (Hannibal Books) and myself. I don't remember what prompted it, but it may well have been his unequalled book *Dius* (2024), with its marvellous cover (fig. 2, p. 174). It shows two fighting birds (a falcon and a heron), which is a detail from the painting *Young Knight in a Landscape* (c. 1510) by Vittore Carpaccio, which Hertmans writes about in this book.

All the writers focused primarily on bird/human relationships in Europe, occasionally allowing themselves to venture beyond, knowing that all cultures have rich literary, mythological, religious and artistic histories in this field. The texts in the book are accompanied by the works on display in the exhibition plus a lot more material. There is no chronological, geographical or thematic order to be found in the publication. We have allowed the texts to flutter freely, as befits birds.

Many thanks to everyone who contributed to this book and the exhibition *BIRDS*, especially Hannibal Books and the Mauritshuis's own magnificent and imperturbable exhibition team, led by Suzan van den Berg van Saparoea. Several names have already been mentioned, but another one needs to be highlighted, that of curator Justine Rinnooy Kan. What a joy it was to develop a concept with you – a concept that took flight early on. And lastly, our sincere thanks go to Adrienne Quarles van Ufford, the curator who temporarily adopted the name 'The Goldfinch' for this exhibition.

This exhibition would not have been possible without the generous support of the VriendenLoterij, Sichting de Johan Maurits Compagnie, our Friends of the Mauritshuis, the Lucas Fonds, Fonds 'De Opzet', Dutch Masters Foundation and the Thurkow Foundation.

On behalf of the Mauritshuis, *The Goldfinch* and Simon Schama, we are also greatly indebted to: Valentijn As, Martin Clayton, Maghiel van Crevel, Laura Cumming, Eric Dereumaux, Gerald Derksen, Emily Ehrman, Tracey Emin, Charlotte La Forêt, Araceli Rojas Martinez Gracida, Manon Henzen, Iris van Herpen, Charly Herscovici, Stefan Hertmans, Auke Florian van Hiemstra, Philip Hoare, Friedell ten Holt-Derksen, Rick Honings, Edwin van Huis, Wilt Lukas Idema, Jan van IJken, Dominika Kasova, Michiel van Kempen, Séan Kissane, Tamara Kostianovsky, Suzanne Lambooy, Bram Langeveld, Louise Lawler, Eva Meijer, Wayne Modest, Markus Müller, Sara Nijssen, Kim Oosterlinck, Aude Raimbault, Pieter Roelofs, Naomi Sanyang, Axel Schering, Margot van Schinkel, Annette Schmidt, Ilona van Tuinen, Matthias Ubl, Marieke Vellekoop, Petra Warrink, Harry Weller and Mariet Westermann.

1 Boussauw 2024, pp. 49–50.

INTRODUCTION

Oh, for the Wings...

Simon Schama

FIG. 1
Owl, c. 40,000–26,000 BCE.
Engraving on rock, 45 cm high.
Salle Hillaire, Chauvet Cave,
Vallon-Pont-d'Arc.

Around 35,000 years ago, give or take a millennium, someone, in the gloom of the Pont d'Arc caves at Chauvet, felt the need for the company of an owl. So that someone took a bone or a flint, and scratched one into the limestone wall (fig. 1). There it perches, unmistakeably owlish: wings neatly tucked, tufty-eared, motionless, watchful. Discovered in 1994, it is the earliest known image of a bird, and one of the few appearing in Paleolithic art, dominated as that was by hoofed quadrupeds. But here is an owl, perhaps already imagined as guardian-protector, alert to the presence of peril, since, after all, the nocturnal bird could see when the caves went dark, and humans, for the most part, could not.

Fast forward 20,000 years to the decoration of the caves at Lascaux, and here are a pair of birds, facing in opposite directions. The little songbird is described by the shorthand profile familiar to the illustrators of children's books and the icon designers of Twitter. But above, or beside it, depending on your point of view, is a bird of another feather entirely: a man-bird or bird-man, its beaked head set atop a human body, albeit one whose arms are outstretched diagonally, in the manner of unfolded wings. Even at the dawn of culture, then, the imagination of *Homo sapiens* was taking flight.

Since then, virtually every human culture, in some form or other, has turned bird-catcher: for food, for sport, for instruments of writing and the plumage of vanity that supplies airs and graces. Since roughly fashioned flutes were the first musical instruments to be discovered in Ice Age caves, the inspiration for paleo-music may have been the song of birds that greeted our distant forbears when they emerged from their stone shelters. Birds are Jurassic descendants, and for seers and poets, not just a particular arrangement of bones and feathers, but metaphysical message-carriers, from the domain of the gods. 'Hail to thee, blithe Spirit/ Bird thou never wert,' Shelley insists, hymning the skylark, 'That from Heaven or near it/ Pourest thy full heart.' (p. 183). When mortals imagined human-looking intermediaries between themselves and the immortals, they instinctively supplied them with wings. If the fate of our gross bodies was to crumble into the receiving earth, our spirit selves did what birds routinely do – ascend – into the paradise humans conjure from the optical infinity of the sky. Some religions – Nepalese Vajrayana Buddhists and Zoroastrian Parsi – ensure that consolatory ascent by having white-backed or slender-billed vultures consume human corpses laid out for them atop stone *dakhma,* so that the remains of the dead rise into the heavens within the bellies of the scavenging birds. One of the standing stones at the earliest known temple, at the Neolithic site of Göbekli Tepi in Upper Mesopotamia (now Turkey), has the familiar profile of a vulture, leading some archaeologists to believe that this may have been the way the dead were disposed of 11,000 years ago. Now, in India, this ancient rite of inter-species recycling has been precluded by the near extinction of millions of vultures that have consumed the anti-inflammatory drug diclofenac along with the carcasses of cattle that have been indiscriminately dosed with the drug.

No other creatures have fixed themselves so obsessively and ubiquitously in our restless, earth-stuck imaginations, the fixation painted, imprinted, sculpted, filmed in our art. They can appear as terminal destroyers or primordial creators, or first the one, and then the other. They have featured in high art as agents of torture, shredding the innards of presumptuous, fire-questing Prometheus. And birds have been sexualised, at least when Jupiter was said to have disguised himself as a swan and – this stretches the imagination, even for readers of Ovid – after some feathery foreplay, copulated with the Queen of Sparta. Out of the resulting egg hatched not a damp cygnet, but Helen, whose beauty would swerve history and doom Troy.

Unless the bird is flightless, or unless (as has happened) a camera can be attached to the legs of migrating geese, the inner motions of the avian flock, their social orchestration, remain elusive to humans; confined as we are for the most part, to distant observation. There is one great exception, however: the Galapagos Islands where Darwin's finches revealed to him the biologically transforming truth of natural selection. On those islands one may tactfully walk amid nesting flocks in their thousands, without the birds bolting, scattering or flying up in alarm, for humans, in the recent past at least, have never come among them as predators, or robbers of eggs. And so, one makes one's way between their nests, incredulously, as if admitted to a prelapsarian Eden.

Elsewhere, the tantalising elusiveness of birds, their evasion from our reach, has challenged the arts (which are, after all, in the business of fixing the impermanent) to nail down their presence. Hence, at this historically alarming moment of global bird population collapse, this little finch-sized exhibition: a visual document, across media and the ages, of the intertwining of human and avian destinies.

FIG. 2 (Cat. 1, p. 45)
Carel Fabritius, *The Goldfinch*, 1654. Oil on panel, 33.5 × 22.8 cm. Mauritshuis, The Hague.

The two masterworks bookending the show attempt, in their radically different ways, to come as close as they can to the essential vitality of bird-life: one in a tone of sympathetic tenderness, the other in a state of euphoric uplift. But the lifelikeness of Carel Fabritius's painting is conditional on captivity, while that of Constantin Brancusi's sculpture presupposes the release of flight (fig. 2 and 3).

If truth to life is measured by likeness, then *The Goldfinch,* painted by Carel Fabritius (1622–1654) in the year of the gunpowder explosion in Delft that took the artist's life (along with, one assumes, that of his model bird) has no peer in the aviary of images. Was it the fact that nature had already so splashily painted the bird that caught Fabritius's attention? Or was it the opportunity to make the ultimate case for the illusionistic power of painting, since, as Linda Stone-Ferrier has argued, the picture could have been set in a jamb of the ground-floor window of a Delft house, so that the plaster background of the painting would dissolve into the actual plaster filling of the jamb. The idea would have been to deceive passers-by, accustomed as they were to seeing pet birds, many of them caged near open windows and which were a commonplace of town life, into thinking – as we might ourselves – that there is an actual, live, goldfinch. One, moreover, with which we exchange looks. The bird is in three-quarter profile as if turned towards us, or indeed past us, into the aerial space forever denied him.

All portrait painters ask, or more often, require, stillness from their subjects. Fabritius's feathered sitter has no option. Anyone who has watched goldfinches at the feeder or in the wild, knows that, like other finches that move in social flocks, they are among the most restive of small songbirds. The word flutter might have been coined for them; and in breeding season, autumn and winter, combative with each other too, as might be expected. Feathers have been known to fly; but if they are to be accurately drawn, the fluttering and the flying have to be chained out of them. By separating the bird from his flock, Fabritius has made a creature serviceable for his virtuosity. He has created a masterpiece by capturing a captivity. Does he acknowledge this? Is there a calculated, even theatrical, air of solitary wistfulness about the goldfinch: that cast shadow, so emotionally showy? And does this loneliness trigger thoughts of another solitude: that of the Saviour on whose crown of thorns the finch is traditionally said to have alighted, splashing its face with the blood that forever after identified its kind. Sacred ornithology aside, this bird's back is turned away from the feeder and thus away from the tricks of servile obedience with seed and water that pet goldfinches were trained to perform for human entertainment. Perched on the very edge of the canister, robbed of freedom, he is indifferent to performance, even for Fabritius, since the characteristic that makes most birds birds – flight – is no longer his to command.

FIG. 3 (Cat. 37, p. 121)
Constantin Brancusi, *L'Oiseau dans l'espace* (Bird in Space), 1932–1940. Brass, 151 cm high. Peggy Guggenheim Collection, Venice.

Suppose, though, that art is relieved of the obligation of likeness; of measuring its art-fullness by verisimilitude: the literalism that Brancusi (1876–1957) dismissed, high-handedly, as mere duplication? Instead, his self-imposed mission was to lend visible, tactile form to an abstract *idea*: in particular, that of his perpetual obsession: the ecstasy of flight. 'All my life,' he wrote, 'I have searched for the essence of flight. Flight! What happiness!' But here, too, is an obvious difficulty: the challenge of embodying liberated motion in a fixed object. The paradoxical mission Brancusi set himself over 30 years, then, was to create a form that would appear to escape the solid materials from which it was constructed, even as he sought to retain the material qualities of wood, marble or bronze (fig. 3). Hours, days, would be spent in the toil of polish and burnish. All that work was done in an effort to have his birds seem to break loose from their base, the better to give a sensation of kinetic energy, the rush of released ascent. If he could achieve that – and for what it's worth, I believe he did – then the idea-subject might be said to govern the demonstration of art, not vice versa. And the quality that gives most birds their mammalian distinctiveness – aerial freedom – could be said to have been restored.

Whether or not the artist had succeeded in materialising the exhilaration of unbounded flight, however, was not the first question put to Brancusi's champions at an extraordinary trial in 1927–28, which tested whether his *Bird in Space* could be thought of as a piece of art, and thus free of customs duty, or as a domestic utensil or industrial tool, liable for payment. Forced to cough up on arrival in New York in 1926, the sculptor and chosen witnesses were suing the government to have the amount returned, but, more importantly, to have the sculpture's legitimacy as a work of art vindicated.

Early in the proceedings, the question put by one of the panel of three judges was not, however, about the motion of birds, but the opposite. Apparently, the test of whether the sculpture was art was its power to persuade a beholder that it was a proper target to be shot.

> October 21st, 1927. In the case of C Brancusi vs The United States
> ASSOCIATE JUSTICE YOUNG to the witness testifying on behalf of the plaintiff.
> 'If you saw it in the forest, you would not take a shot at it?'
> Witness, EDWARD STEICHEN, photographer, and owner of the sculpture, called for the plaintiff, Mr. Brancusi.
> 'No, Your Honour.'

In other words, this is evidently not the kind of thing that could be mistaken for an actual bird – that is to say, a creature defined entirely by its destiny to be blasted out of the sky, and possibly, like pheasants, grouse or partridge, hatched and raised only so that they could be killed in large numbers for the sporting amusement of the landed classes. And since the definition of art, sculpture in particular, is, as per the US statute of 1913, 'imitations of natural form' ('chiefly' but not exclusively human) and since the object made by Mr Brancusi could not possibly fall under this category, it then follows that said object is not 'art' and thus, as an object 'of utility', possibly industrial, is correctly considered liable to customs revenue as imposed at New York in October 1926, at the rate of 40% *ad valorem*, a sum of $240.

Thus it was that Brancusi and his *Bird in Space* – the one currently in the Seattle Art Museum, but other than the different supports, nearly identical with the Guggenheim Venice version in this exhibition – was drawn into a court debate about what could, or could not be properly judged to be art. Marcel Duchamp had brought the *Bird* from Brancusi's Paris studio, along with 20 other sculptures, for a one-man show he was curating at the Brummer Gallery in New York. But it was Steichen, the owner of the piece, who had to fork over the dollars, though he trusted that Brancusi would reimburse him. When he heard about the imposition, the sculptor was furious, not for the bill, but that the *Bird* should have been judged 'an object of utility' akin to 'a table, kitchen or hospital utensils' in the formula of para 399 of the Tariff Act. On 7 February 1927, Brancusi wrote to Duchamp that he must 'protest energetically because this is a great injustice', meaning that the customs officials had implied that, even if this was not some sort of tool, since there were a number of other, almost identical bird in space sculptures, it followed that Brancusi was operating a production line, akin to the manufacturers of seasonal knick-knacks, and thus still liable. Duchamp and Steichen needed no encouragement to sue the US Customs and Revenue Service. Steichen, sculptor Jacob Epstein, *Vanity Fair* editor Frank Crowninshield, art critic Forbes Watson and William Henry Fox, the director of the Brooklyn Museum, were called as witnesses for the plaintiff.

The judges and attorneys defending the government, presented themselves as plain-spoken regular Americans, bewildered by both the bronze and the man. Who was Mr Brancusi, anyway, they enquired? In fact, he had been famous ever since he had exhibited *The Kiss* and

Mlle Pogany and other works at New York's Armory Show in 1913 in the company of Picasso, Matisse, Van Gogh, Cézanne and Marcel Duchamp. It was there that his work moved a wealthy Irish-American lawyer, John Quinn, to go on to be Brancusi's most impassioned and loyal patron. Quinn visited Brancusi in his Paris studio, and before his death in 1925 had acquired 50 of his works. It was Quinn who had pressed the government for changes to the Tariff Act in 1922 that resulted in duty exemption for works of art and had encouraged shows of Brancusi's work at New York's Wildenstein & Co. and Brummer galleries.

Despite this, the witnesses for Brancusi had to jump through hoops to persuade the judges that a) they knew, professionally, what they were talking about when it came to works of art, and b) that *Bird in Space* really was one. There was a lot of sneering from the bench and the government's lawyers: 'You are a curator or something, you say? Justice Waite asked William Fox, surely with eyebrows raised. 'I am director at the [Brooklyn] museum,' Fox replied with commendable restraint. At times the proceedings descended into the kind of absurdity that anticipated the modernist comedy of Ionesco or Beckett.

> Direct examination (of Forbes Watson)
> Q: Mr Watson, what is your profession?
> A: I edit *The Arts Magazine*
> Q: What is the nature of the magazine?
> A: It is a magazine devoted to art.
> etc.

In his summing up, the senior judge insisted that 'without the exercise of rather a vivid imagination it bears no resemblance to a bird, except perchance, with such imagination it may be likened to the shape of the body of a bird. It has neither head nor feet nor feathers portrayed in the piece. It is entirely smooth on its exterior which is a polished and burnished surface.'

Witnesses for Brancusi did their best to argue that literal resemblance was beside the point. Frank Crowninshield, the editor of *Vanity Fair*, put it best when he said that the piece 'has the suggestion of flight; it suggests grace, aspiration, vigour, coupled with speed, in the spirit of strength, potency, beauty, just as a bird does'. Anticipating, correctly, that the academic sculptors the government would call, in particular Robert Ingersoll Aitken, while admitting he had never actually seen a Brancusi, would, when shown the exhibit, disqualify the *Bird* from being considered a work of art since it did not produce any 'aesthetic emotion', Steichen testified that it did emanate a 'great sense of beauty... that bird gives me the sensation of a rushing bird and that the sculpture's present form was the product of 20 years 'of changing it, dividing it, until it has reached the stage where the lines and form express a bird, the lines suggest flying up in the sky.'

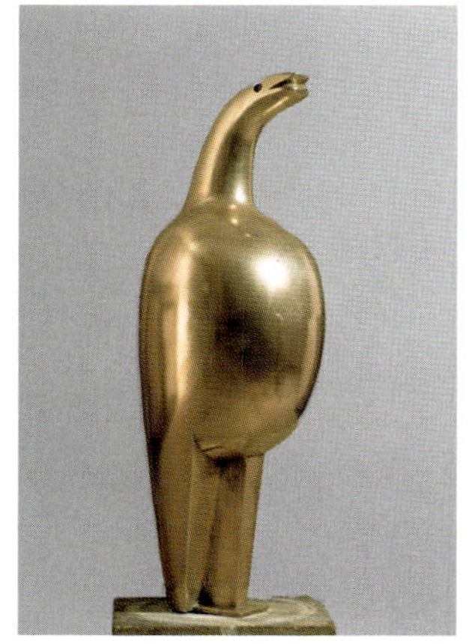

FIG. 4
Contantin Brancusi, *Maiastra* (Master), c. 1912. Bronze, 63 cm high. Palazzo Venier dei Leoni, Venice.

Steichen was alluding to the long history of Brancusi's immersion in Romanian folklore around the *maïastra*: golden birds with powers of transformation and resurrection; versions of which, in a multitude of stories, survived across northern Europe and were especially strong in the Slav countries of the east. Though Brancusi had begun to brood on those birds, the first performance in 1910 of Stravinsky's *Firebird* by Diaghilev's Ballet Russes in Paris, where the sculptor had lived since 1904, quickened his creative fixation. That resulted – eventually – in a series of Maiastra sculptures, in white and yellow marble as well as polished bronze (fig. 4). Much of the commentary on them has been concerned to point out the (blindingly obvious) phallic form of the bird's neck while passing over Brancusi's attempt, in the open beak, inflated breast and erect posture, to embody the other legendary attribute of the *maïastra*: its song, said to surpass any other earthly music. And though Brancusi continued to make his birds in marble, it was the bronzes that caught (often literally when he photographed them) the light that proclaimed another characteristic of the golden creatures: their solar power in reflecting or transmitting the radiance of the sun, and thus acting as both bringers of light, and enablers of the resurrection of life. By 1923, the sculptor had changed his vision of what most embodied the transcendent power of bird life from the music they made to the force of their flight.

In the end, Justice Waite found for Brancusi, albeit grudgingly, conceding that 'there has been developing a so-called new school of art, whose exponents attempt to portray abstract ideas rather than to imitate natural objects. Whether or not we are in sympathy with these newer ideas, we think the facts of their existence and their influence upon the art world as recognised by the courts must be considered.'

Brancusi's *Bird* was vindicated, the $240 returned. A New York tabloid printed a photograph of the sculpture with the facetiously shouty headline 'It's a BIRD!'

Brancusi, you might say, is on the side of birds, in a way that, for example, Jan Baptist Weenix (1621–1659), whose large game pieces depended on not just stillness, but an aesthetic of disarticulated death, is evidently not. Joshua Reynolds, who preferred his subjects lively, offered, in his lapidary manner, the most economical verdict on the painter, when he recorded an entry in the journal of his 1781 Dutch art tour (and I think we can infer the heavy sigh): 'Another dead swan by Weenix.' Unless, of course, the Catholic Weenix was surreptitiously smuggling in so many disguised swan Depositions from the Cross into pictures, whose commercial value more usually depended on flattering the status and the shotguns of his landed patrons (fig. 5). But the electors at Düsseldorf for whom the younger Weenix – also a virtuoso of hunting still lifes for the wealthy and the nobility — worked, had, however, converted once again from Lutheranism to Catholicism. Should those buyers, on the other hand, be Calvinist, Weenix made sure to retain the long, formalised tradition of *vanitas* (reminders of mortality), hence the presence of the Usual Signifying Suspects: overripe peaches (their mould painted with almost egregious skill); roses about to drop their petals; an extinguished tobacco pipe. But these warmed-over items from emblem book symbolism are disingenuously and mechanically assembled. The vital energy of the picture lies in its glossy, morbid exhibitionism, the painterly equivalent of a high-end undertaker's showroom, plus the kind of colossalism that would appeal to baroque grandeur. Hence this orgiastic spectacle presided over by Pan and his mandatory showgirls on the classical relief, all discharged in a floodlit ecstasy of *necro-barocco*, the bird's breast and belly sacrificially exposed; the theatrically extended wing, every feather a flourish of loaded lead white pigment, curling and quivering along the serpentine Line of Beauty. The picture is outrageously alive *because* the bird is so thrillingly dead – and in a torqued pose that none of Tchaikovsky's balletically crumpled swans would ever reproduce. There was at least one painter contrarian enough to put the unvarnished truth of death back into the bloodless translation from living birds to the decoratively dead.

In 1639, Rembrandt (1606–1669) painted a scene that is still unique in the genre of 'still life': the conventional category to which this most unconventional painting is routinely attached (fig. 6). The choice of bird is not arbitrary. Pagan antiquity associated peacocks with immortality, their flesh supposedly resistant to decay. Opportunistically Christianised, the bird became an emblem of the Resurrection and eternal life. No such luck for this pair of peacocks, though, whose mortality is decisively painted with unprecedented candour. 'Game pieces' with hanging dead birds became a commonplace genre in Dutch art, especially in the later seventeenth century when they were sought after by patricians who wished to present themselves as country estate owners, partial to dogs, guns and falling birds and to which the Weenix dynasty, father and son, richly contributed.

On one level, of course, Rembrandt could be said to be painting with naturalistic straightforwardness, since peacocks, like all other game birds, had to be drained before they could be prepared for banqueting spectacle. But the addition of a pensive child violates yet another convention: the necessary absence of all humans from game pieces. The awkward presence is an embarrassment to an assumed norm: the uncontested spell of decorative death, no questions asked. Too bad. The snub-nosed child poses inconvenient questions as curious children will. Am I supposed to like this? The child gazes at the upturned bird, whose claw feet, brightly lit, are attached to a wall hook that suggests the form of a cross. But the body of the second peacock obstructs the child's view of the stream of blood. Only we can see that, as the rivulet of blood flows towards us before falling over the stone ledge.

Even by Rembrandt's standards, this is a wilfully un-beautiful, un-game piece. In the twentieth century it ended up in the collection of Jean-Joseph Marie Chabot, who had lent it to the Rijksmuseum from 1923 to 1942 before selling it, in occupied Amsterdam, to the dealer Ernst Göpel, who bought it for Hitler's intended Führermuseum in Linz, where, had that materialised, it would have been an unlikely focus for a quiet meditation on mortality.

Rembrandt's hanging, bleeding birds have struck a creative chord with successive generations of artists challenging the aestheticisation of animal death. Chaim Soutine (1893–1943) above all, who went from meditative immersion in Rembrandt's hanging bodies to arranging carcasses in his studio and painting them with a thick whirl of paint that suggested thrashing vitality before the translation into 'still life' (figs. 7 and 8).

Tamara Kostianovsky (b. 1974), the daughter of a plastic surgeon, grew up in Argentina during the era of military rule when humans were hunted and made to disappear. The country has possibly the most carnivorous diet in the world, so it was impossible to avoid the spectacle of butchered, hanging carcasses, birds or beasts. The Argentinian style of barbecuing a whole animal on a frame (not unlike a music stand or an easel), spreadeagling the body, was bound to trigger thoughts of sacrifice, sacred or profane. Interest through her father's profession of what lay beneath the dermis might have been registered in painting, had it not been for a time of sudden, personal difficulty. Kostianovsky arrived in New York in 2000 exactly at the point when the Argentinian economy and currency collapsed, leaving her without the means to buy canvas, pigment and the rest. She turned instead to her wardrobe, to clothes she had stopped wearing but not yet thrown away: T-shirts, jeans, scarves, jackets, whatever came to hand, also discarded cushion covers, upholstery, towelling, bed linen. With a specific subject in mind, these textiles, cut, shredded, restitched, would be the makings of her art. But it was the next step, so counter-intuitive, that would create her striking originality. The repurposed fabrics were, by definition, domestic, personal, sometimes intimate; many of them in the bright colours and printed patterns of dress or domestic interiors. Using them for bloodied carcasses, including exposed or trailing viscera (or in another project, the brutally exposed rings of tree stumps), was both a move that could simply collapse under the weight of its incongruousness, or – as it turned out – an inspired turn that brings together slaughter and comfort (fig. 9).

Which of course is what Weenix's game pieces do, but by erasing any physical signs of a kill in favour of the polished aesthetic of the ornamental trophy. Breaking the illusion, Kostianovsky restores the bloodying. Violently made wounds gape, viscera poke through the openings, but every bit of the carnage is executed in materials that, but for their shredding into remnants, could be fabric available for online shopping. Somehow the exposure of just what it takes to feed consumer tastes and appetites, rendered in the materials of our daily comfort, makes that acknowledgement all the more painful.

Big Vulture multiplies these colliding sensibilities. The dead bird was itself nourished from the dead. A length of pale fabric describes the naked neck of the vulture, famously fixated on cleaning itself after a carrion feed. The dark shreds that make up its feathers suggest the preening that takes up much of its day. But one of the wings – of a span that is the widest of any bird in the world – is broken. The knowledge that there are currently just 500 or so condors left in the wild somehow piles on the dismay. And Kostianovsky seems to have made this particular bird a ragged, rag-made faux-creature. That something nonetheless *is* being renewed, namely the textile strips that have been saved from the landfill and turned into questions about how we look at the death of other species, only makes that self-interrogation more acute. This is, inter alia, what strong art is supposed to do.

It is, of course, anachronistic to think that the original subscribers to the folio edition of *The Birds of America* by John James Audubon (1785–1851), the first volume (of five) appearing in London in 1827, would have thought that killing the subjects in order to lend his plates maximum life was in any way paradoxical or cruel. That the observed bird was dead was a given condition of its illustration. Audubon's predecessor, Alexander Wilson (1766–1813), who illustrated

FIG. 5 (Cat. 11, p. 72) Jan Weenix, *Dead Swan*, 1716. Oil on canvas, 173 × 154 cm. Museum Boijmans Van Beuningen, Rotterdam.

FIG. 6 (Cat. 10, pp. 70–71) Rembrandt, *Still Life with Peacocks*, c. 1639. Oil on canvas, 145 × 135.5 cm. Rijksmuseum, Amsterdam.

FIG. 7
Rembrandt, *Deposition of Christ*, c. 1632–1633. Oil on panel, 89.4 × 65.2 cm. Alte Pinakothek, Munich.

FIG. 8
Chaïm Soutine, *Dead Fowl*, 1926. Oil on canvas, 97.5 × 63.3 cm. Joseph Winterbotham Collection, Art Institute Chicago.

FIG. 9 (Cat. 18, p. 85)
Tamara Kostianovsky, *Big Vulture*, 2016. Discarded and recycled textiles, 132 × 218 × 135 cm. Courtesy RX&SLAG, Paris/New York.

268 species in his *American Ornithology,* drew live birds when he could sketch without disturbing them but resorted to freshly killed ones when this was impractical. When Audubon was in Boston in 1833 looking for a golden eagle to draw, he discussed with his doctor George Parkman (who would himself be murdered by a Harvard professor of chemistry fifteen years later) the best means of killing such a large bird without doing damage to its plumage (fig. 10).

Drawing the wild bird in some dramatic pose, like a kill, amid the landscape or seascape that sustained it was what distinguished Audubon's images from traditional European ornithologies that displayed them without habitat, as if they were already (as they were) detached scientific specimens. Audubon was after the bird in its full, living nature, and did all he could to document that nature: stalking and noting the behaviour of waterfowl, raptors, common backyard songsters, making copious notes not just of the birds themselves but of their habitat; whether or not they lived in flocks, mated pairs or alone, until he had the richest possible picture of their habits.

But the golden eagle was most abundant in the country west of the Rockies where Audubon had never set foot, and he had to rely on a bird trapped in New Hampshire and sold to him in Boston. How to kill it then with least damage, and also, to give Audubon his due, with minimal pain? The choice was between gassing the bird with a mix of carbon dioxide and carbon monoxide given off by a coal fire, or electrocution, which Audubon was eager to try but had to abandon for lack of a battery big enough to kill the eagle with one decisive bolt.

What followed was a tragic farce. Audubon imagined a bond between man and bird, especially this one that made such strong eye contact. At times he thought of freeing the eagle, thinking 'how pleasing it would be to see him spread out his broad wings and sail away towards the rocks of his wild haunts', but then 'someone seemed to whisper that I ought to take a portrait of this magnificent bird' and he returned to his plan of execution.

A heavy blanket was thrown over the cage; a coal fire was lit. For his own safety Audubon exited the room, waiting next door 'to hear him fall down from his perch, but after listening for *hours* [his emphasis]', he went to the cage, lifted the blankets and there the bird was very much alive 'with his bright unflinching eye turned towards me, and as lively and vigorous as ever.' He subjected the eagle to the same treatment the next day with smoke so thick it was more likely to kill the household than the bird. And since it was too big 'to throttle... I thrust a long, pointed piece of steel through his heart when my proud prisoner instantly fell dead without even ruffling a feather.'

The dead eagle was quickly pinned in the theatrical pose Audubon wanted: set against snow-covered mountains (lifted from his hero Jacques-Louis David's portrait of Bonaparte crossing the Alps); the bird, its beak open as if emitting a cry of triumph, flies upwards with a hare in its grip. As if inspired by the new genre of Gothic horror, Audubon adds a gruesome detail. A talon punctures the left eye of the hare, from which blood is already leaking. In the original drawing, Audubon gave himself a background walk-on as a figure crossing a perilously sloping wooden bridge slung between two peaks. The print retains the bridge, but Audubon, imagined witness to the kill and the flight, has vanished.

A 19-year-old Charles Darwin heard Audubon lecture in Edinburgh when he was briefly a medical student there, and the ornithologist's best biographer, Richard Rhodes, believes that the student might have been impressed by the American's painstaking attention to anatomical and behavioural detail in each species he had observed. *Birds of America* and the textual volumes *American Ornithology* appeared when Romanticism and the sentimentalising of birds was making way for a drier-eyed, more factual account of the natural world. The violence of raptors was becoming seen as part of the natural order in which stronger beasts preyed on the weaker.

Though there had been a demand for pictures of epic animal fights – lions attacking horses for example – for centuries, the spectacle of avian violence never really had much of a market in the nineteenth century, devoted as the middle class still was to Shelley's metaphysical ode to the skylark.

FIG. 10
John James Audubon, *Golden Eagle*, from *The Birds of America*, 1827–1838. Hand-coloured aquatint from *The Birds of America*, vol. 2, plate 181. Teylers Museum, Haarlem.

FIG. 11
Edwin Landseer, *Hawking in the Olden Time*, 1832. Oil on canvas, 153 × 184 cm. Kenwood House, London.

With one exception, Edwin Landseer's painting *Hawking in the Olden Time*: a mid-air kill, so shockingly unsparing, that, compositionally, it has no precedent and no successors in bird depiction, not just in Britain where it was created, but anywhere else before or since (fig. 11). In his essay (p. 172) on the Venetian painter Vittore Carpaccio and his *Young Knight in a Landscape*, Stefan Hertmans brilliantly discusses the same violent subject of a heron attacked by a falcon and its meaning for the subject. But the two paintings are contrasts in man-bird dramatisations. As you would expect in a Renaissance painting, Carpaccio has set the attack in the background and separated the raptor from the hunted. The bird action speaks to the knightly vocation. By contrast, the English masterpiece sets the moment of lethal impact at the front of the picture space, overwhelming everything else. The falconers are just add-on historical props. The kill is the action; the story, the painting. Its creator was the most unlikely dramatist of aerial horror: Edwin Landseer (1802–1873). Because he is usually thought of as *Sir* Edwin, Queen Victoria's favourite, the producer of chocolate-box maudlin sentimentality, starving villagers, the *Monarch of the Glen* – a Highland stag so majestic it was bound to make Her Majesty's heart beat faster, and especially dog portraits (in one case, *Laying Down the Law*, with assorted canine species dressed as judges and lawyers), this huge painting has gone largely unnoticed, not only as a nearly impossible composition but one executed with the unsparing psychological intensity that we associate with modernism's transcriptions of nightmares. Which, without over-determining the case, may actually have been true, since Landseer suffered the first of what would become a succession of mental breakdowns, possibly consistent with bipolarity, that he held at bay only by resorting to heavy doses of opium and alcohol. In the end they consumed him and what was left of his sanity, so that the most famous painter in Britain died in a mental asylum in his early seventies.

The painting does what photography in its early years could not: capture a split-second of attack, suspended in air and time. The imploding aerial mess of wings, bones and feathers is so violent and disorderly that it takes a little while to get a clear reading of the event. Inferred speed through light – that vast, wide-open, pearly expanse of sky – is essential to the brutal drama. A peregrine falcon, such as this one, can drop from its sky-high point of observation on to a prey at speeds bordering 390 kilometres an hour. This one has done just that, landing on a much bigger quarry: a grey heron. The heron is much bigger but in frantic shock. The falcon's wings are still open and extended, one of them painted at 90 degrees to the picture plane, lending the attack its frightening muscle. The beak of the raptor is already pinned on to the body of its quarry which has been turned upside down, stalky legs poking into the sky while it thrashes desperately to free itself from the killer's grip.

FIG. 12 (Cat. 12, p. 73)
Hans Holbein the Younger, *Portrait of Robert Cheseman (1485–1547)*, 1533. Oil on panel, 58.8 × 62.8 cm. Mauritshuis, The Hague.

This is not the traditional way in which art served falconers and falconry. The glorious portrait of Robert Cheseman by Hans Holbein (1497/98–1543) might have served to promote his social credentials from the manor-owning commoner whose father had been Keeper of the Wardrobe to Henry VII to a much more elevated status (fig. 12). The painting succeeded in so far as it has given the impression that Cheseman was Chief Falconer to Henry VIII, but no documentary evidence other than the picture supports this. The persuasiveness lies in the painting's order, the heads of both handler and hooded bird turned in the same direction as if some sound has triggered their attention.

Falconers are included in Landseer's enormous painting but in Romantically imagined supporters' roles, dressed in loosely imagined late medieval costume. There is an element of human mastery in the lead extending from the upraised arm of the falconer to another falcon, but all this is secondary to the violent sensation in the foreground. Surprisingly, perhaps (or not, given the relatively primitive and pain-inducing state of the profession), the painting was executed in 1832, for a successful London dentist. It was shown at the Royal Academy's annual exhibition, and then sold for the substantial sums of £3,000 to a succession of buyers, ending up with the Guinness family at Kenwood House, near Hampstead Heath in north-west London.

As far as art is concerned, then, birds keep close company with death. Not invariably though. A counter tradition invokes them as harbingers of new life, a second life, or even life eternal. Possibly the most telling moment in the 'What is art?' trial was when Jacob Epstein was asked by one of the government lawyers if Brancusi was not 'isolated' (meaning, incomprehensibly *outré*) in his efforts? To this line of questioning, Epstein replied firmly: 'No, he is related to a very ancient form of sculpture. He does not stand absolutely alone. He is related to the ancient sculptures like the early Egyptian of 3,000 years old', and then announced that he would bring illustrations of his contention. Off he went, outside the court, to do just that. 'This,' Epstein said, on returning, dramatically flourishing his photograph, 'is an ancient Egyptian hawk, 3,000 years ago.' Startled, Justice Waite asked him if that was really, for him, a recognisable hawk? 'An ornithologist might not see it. ...the feathers are not shown, the feet are not shown... still you get the impression it is a hawk?' 'Yes,' said Epstein, firmly. The transcript does not specify the image, but evidently it had the unsettling effect of turning the government's case on its head by replacing the traditionalist objection that Brancusi was some sort of incomprehensible modernist eccentric with the observation that he was actually drawing on ancient practices that had little to do with literalist representation, but yet were rooted in the most ancient civilisations.

Epstein's photo was, literally, an illustration of the universalism of the human fixation with the bird world, through millennia of time, and in every known cultural space. It is this shared obsession, the deep wish not just to observe birds, but actually partake of their powers and mysteries, to the point of generating hybrids, half avian, half human; sometimes as in Egyptian images of Horus, creatures with the heads of birds and the bodies of men, or in ancient Mesopotamia and Persia, winged animals with human heads. In competitive dialogue with the aesthetics of avian death is the opposite tradition, which sees them as integral to the resurrection of light. Their reappearance in spring accompanied by a chorus of song is a sign that all is well with the natural roll-around of the seasons, and the human place in them. Chaucer begins his *Tales* told by Canterbury pilgrims in the vernal month of Aprille, when nature's remaking of the world is greeted by 'smale foweles maken melodye/ That slepen all the nyght with open ye'. In the Hebrew Bible it is the post-diluvian return of a dove to Noah's ark, an olive leaf in its beak, that signifies the resurrection of the world.

And if birds may be the carriers of good news, and their lives, however brief, somehow tied up, like the phoenix, with perpetual renewal, then why should mankind not imagine divinity as avian and yearn to strap on, or otherwise evolve, wings. Hybrid man-birds occur in almost all creation myths, the glaring exception being the first chapter of the Hebrew book of Genesis in which the appearance of both creatures of the marine deep and 'fowls that may fly above the earth' (Genesis 1:20, in the King James Version) is the unguided act of a formless deity. But verse 20 makes the crucial connection between the altitude of flight and proximity to 'the open firmament of heaven' that would sacralise two birds: the dove returning to Noah's ark a second time with a leaf from an olive tree in its beak (Genesis 8:11), signifying the retreat of the waters and the post-diluvian rebirth of the world, and the dove-form taken by the Holy Spirit in Christian tradition, occasionally at the Annunciation, almost always at the Resurrection.

In almost every other religion, birds participate decisively in the act of cosmic creation. The most ancient Egyptian creation myth has a bird, usually a heron, laying an egg on the mound that has risen from the primordial waters of Nun. From that egg the sun is hatched, and with the accomplishment of its diurnal course, life on earth can begin. The *ba*, a human-headed, bird-bodied deity, is sometimes characterised as 'soul', but its role in the cosmic order of ancient Egypt is more poetically complex (cat. 45, p. 138). It represents the spirit, allowing the immaterial element of the body, after death, to ascend to the sun, and accompany it on its daily journey, returning at night to the gross matter of the corpse lying entombed in the netherworld. But the *ba* needs the temporary reunion of spirit and corpse for the dawn of the next day to rise. Versions of this myth, especially the intermediary role of a sacred bird or bird-like creature flying freely between the light of the sun and the darkness of the dead, exist almost everywhere from Hindu India to Zoroastrian Persia and Buddhist South and East Asia. Together they reflect the

FIG. 13 (Cat. 43, p. 136)
Mummified falcon,
Egypt and Nubia, 304–30 BCE.
Organic material, linen,
stucco, polychromy,
52 × 9.5 × 8.1 cm. Rijksmuseum
van Oudheden, Leiden.

deep-rooted human horror of the terminal absoluteness of death. The bird-enabled flight of the immaterial spirit conveys, then, consoling immortality. Upwards lies paradise with the courier birds, or in the Christian version, winged human-adjacent forms called angels, who open the gates to eternal life.

Post-creation mythologies of heroic power and virtue – from pre-Columbian America to Africa and Asia – almost always characterise the life-giving radiance of the sun as a bird-form. In ancient Egypt, the Horus divinity with its falcon head and muscular human body was everywhere. Though always associated with the power and justice-dealing of the pharaohs, the cult of the lanner falcon extended to anyone who could afford to present a mummified bird to priests, so that their dead might be vouchsafed flight to the upper world (fig. 13). Since the birds were indispensable to that migration to eternity, their mummification was as fastidiously executed as that of human bodies. Oil, resin and beeswax were applied to their bodies; their wings and feet neatly tucked in before the linen bands were tightly applied. Mummified birds, mostly dating from the Late/Ptolemaic period, have been found by their thousands in excavations throughout Upper and Lower Egypt. Some of the raptors were selected for pharaonic or aristocratic service so that their death and burial became occasion for vast and elaborate ceremonies.

But all this elaborate sacralisation, the translation into divinities that could determine the fate of otherwise mortal humans, took place at the same time that birds – especially waterfowl such as geese and ducks – were eaten, especially during the spring and autumn seasons when the Nile valley became a vast fluvial lagoon, teeming with millions of waterfowl. When Egypt became integrated into the Greek and Roman worlds, European birds – doves and pigeons – became popular in the Egyptian diet. So a cultural pattern was established in which, at the same time that bird species such as the ibis (sacred to Thoth) and falcon were worshipped and took hybrid forms in which human and avian were indivisible, vast numbers of other species were either caught (fowling expeditions often featured on tomb decoration) or domesticated for local consumption. Occasionally, plucked table birds were interred along with the dead to ensure they would be well fed in the afterlife.

Thus, the toothsome dove, impaled and roasted over. an open flame, without which no classical Lucullan feast would be complete, could reappear in Christian Rome as the immortal Holy Spirit. From the fourth century on, scenes of the Annunciation, the Resurrection and occasionally the Assumption of the Virgin included the Holy Spirit, invariably in the shape of an unblemished dove: at once a consolation for suffering and an augury of new life. Which is why, with the formal theology removed, Henri Matisse (1869–1954) in his wheelchair years needed to have the flutter and coo of doves about his person.

Matisse's first doves were bought in 1936 from a bird vendor on the *quais* by the Seine, but when, with the coming of war, he moved back to the Côte d'Azur, the doves went with him. But not Amélie, his wife of 41 years from whom he was now estranged. Jealous of Lydia Delectorskaya, his assistant, muse and workmate, Amélie had issued a 'her or me' ultimatum. Matisse chose his wife and dismissed Delectorskaya, who in anguish tried to shoot herself in the chest. In pity and his own particular kind of love, Matisse took her back. So there they were: the artist, the brilliantly organising muse and the birds making the way through war-traumatised France, settling briefly at Nice, and then re-establishing a studio home at the Villa le Rêve in St Paul-de Vence eighteen kilometres inland. There, the aviary became more populated as more birds hatched and still more were bought. In 1944, artist and birds were visited by the photographer Henri Cartier-Bresson (1908–2004), who had been taken prisoner in 1940, escaping on his third try in 1943, and joining an underground organisation assisting similarly escaped POWs. While he was himself in hiding, the publisher Pierre Braun commissioned Cartier-Bresson to photograph artists at work for a book to be called *Studio*. That book never happened, but it brought the photographer to Vence. Wonderful images resulted, the most touching of which included the white doves: three of them perching on the roof of their cage (fig. 14); another extraordinary one of the artist tenderly holding a bird in one hand drawing its likeness with the other, the eyes of artist and feathered model locked together.

For Matisse, the company of his doves offered him respite from personal pain and the cruelties of history, which is to say, the traditional gift that doves were thought to bestow: the coming of peace and the chance of new life. The pain was, to begin with, physical. Matisse had been diagnosed with stomach cancer in 1941 for which he had undergone two traumatic surgeries, the second, in 1943, resulting from the incomplete work of the first. The operations left him severely disabled, mostly house-bound, always chair-bound and sometimes bed-bound. Somehow the peace brought by the doves extended to the cat that Matisse also kept close, and that intermittent serenity was all the more craved on discovering that his daughter Marguerite, who had gone missing, had joined the Resistance; been captured, tortured by the Gestapo and then sent to the horrific concentration camp of Ravensbrück. As it turned out, the transport offered an opportunity for escape, but one of the utmost peril. Marguerite jumped from the train deporting her, survived, and in 1945 was reunited with her father.

FIG. 14 (Cat. 47, p. 140)
Henri Cartier-Bresson, *Henri Matisse in His Studio (Vence)*, 1944. Gelatin silver print, 23.7 × 35.8 cm. Fondation Cartier-Bresson, Paris.

That reunion was intense. Marguerite was the child of Matisse's lover before he married: Caroline Joblaud. Accepted by Amélie, Marguerite had regularly posed for her father from childhood until their estrangement in the 1930s. The *papiers découpés,* cut, painted paper – the stunning new art form he invented from his chair and bed – represented the essentialism of children's experiences, ostensibly simple but poetically complex, and included, of course, birds in flight (fig. 15). You hope that Charlie Parker knew *Jazz,* the book of cut-outs that was one of the artist's supreme achievements, since the saxophonist would become the 'Bird' of bebop, a jokey nickname that stuck after he had run over a yardbird chicken while touring down south, optimistically presenting the roadkill to a local host to stew for the band's supper.

In 1946, Matisse gave one of his birds to his rival and friend Pablo Picasso (1881–1973), then paying a visit to Le Rêve together with his new paramour, the painter Françoise Gilot. The bird, as the older artist well knew, had deep familial meaning for Picasso. As a child he had watched his father, the painter and school art teacher José Ruiz Blasco, known as 'El Palomero' (the pigeon fancier) draw one of the rock doves he bred and kept in a dovecot at the family house in Malaga. When Pablito, at the age of eight, showed precocious talent, his father taught him the right way to represent birds. The boy loved the rock doves he saw roosting in the

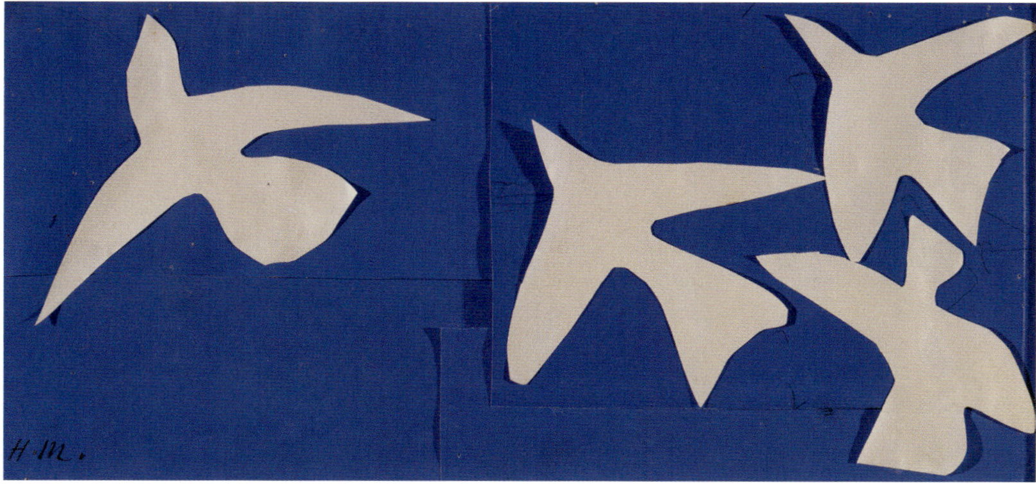

FIG. 15
Henri Matisse, *Jazz (Les oiseaux)* (Jazz [The Birds]), 1947.
Gouache, ink and collage on paper, 200 × 440 mm. Private collection.

sycamore trees of the Plaza de la Merced, made drawings of them in the sand with a stick and, outraging his teachers, would take one to school to sketch instead of doing his assigned work.

But, of course, the gift also represented more than a sentimental memory of El Palomero; it was also a sign of the peace that had settled over the old rivalry and mutual obsession, born of both envy and admiration, both inspiring and exhausting, that held between the two makers of modernism. By 1946, Matisse had come to think of his relationship with the younger artist as paternal, calling him 'the kid' (*le gosse*). Picasso preferred to think of them as brothers-in-art and took the gift as a gesture of mutual respect. After Matisse died in 1954, Picasso wrote that 'Matisse's dove' [meaning the gift] was a beautiful creature – its gentle presence stayed with me. When I drew the dove for the World Peace Congress I was thinking both of the bird itself but also the shared camaraderie between artists.'

FIG. 16
Pablo Picasso, *La colombe de la paix* (Dove of Peace), c. 1950. Pastel on paper, 230 × 310 mm. Germaine Henry and Robert Thomas Collection, Paris.

The pastel drawing of the Peace Dove, 'drawn,' Picasso wrote, while acknowledging Matisse's gift as his model, 'with clean, flowing lines, emphasises simplicity because peace itself should not be complicated' (fig. 16). But the peace embodied in the bird was the kind that Soviet world propaganda liked to pretend it supported following the end of the war against Germany. Influenced by his literary friends André Breton and Louis Aragon, but moved by anti-fascist passions since publishing *The Dream and Lie of Franco* and painting the eternal masterpiece of *Guernica*, Picasso had joined the French Communist Party in October 1944. He would keep the faith, or at least his Party card, until Soviet tanks came to Budapest in 1956.

It was Louis Aragon, poet and fictionalising biographer of Matisse, who, seeing an image of a dove in Picasso's studio (perhaps this one), had the notion of using some similar image as the publicity emblem of the first World Peace Congress to be held in Paris in 1949.

At the height of his comrade phase, Picasso readily agreed and produced an exquisite lithograph, initially in five artist's proofs and 50 prints (fig. 17). Ostensibly simple – as befitted the Communist Party, which, Stalinist purges and Gulag notwithstanding, claimed to represent the world's workers – it is one of the most economically majestic of all Picasso's images, probably winning more immediate converts when it was turned into a poster than *Guernica*. The wispy little crest of feathers at the back of the bird's head is the mark of Picasso's polemical genius since they imply a gust from the winds of war forever blowing in the dark ground that makes the purity of the dove all the more potent, at one and the same time, vulnerable yet inexorable. The bird is, as it had been since the Jewish epic of the Flood and the earliest years of Christian iconography, a herald of the world's rebirth, the sacred symbol of the new church of the proletariat. Never has a more beautiful image been put to work for such a meretricious and atrocious tyranny. But Picasso, when he showed up in person at the Peace Congress held in Sheffield the next year, made it clear that his true allegiance was to the admirable hope of peace. When his and Francoise's daughter was born, a day before the Paris Congress was due to open, it was only natural that they should call her Paloma, the dove.

FIG. 17 (Cat. 48, p. 141)
Pablo Picasso, *La colombe* (The Dove), 1949. Lithography on zinc, 546 × 691 mm. Picasso Museum – Die Sammlung Huizinga, Münster.

In 1957, living in Cannes, Picasso painted a view over the Mediterranean from inside an arched opening that recalled, in homage to Matisse, the older artist's views over the bay at Tangiers (fig. 18). But at the edge of the picture, necessarily, were doves, perching, nesting, pecking, fluttering their feathers, or sitting pat, the way both painters loved them.

There was another bird that, for some years, roosted not just in Picasso's creative imagination, but in his living quarters. In 1946, the same year as his visit to Matisse, Picasso spent six months living in Antibes, working in the studio space at the Palace Grimaldi organised for him by the photographer and sculptor Michel Sima. Surprisingly, since no one had been allowed this privilege other than Dora Maar during the creation of *Guernica*, Picasso asked Sima to make a photographic record of him at work. Sima's precious archive includes a wonderful portrait of the artist holding a little owl in the palm of his left hand (fig. 19). If the painter looks a bit tense, it may be because 'Ubu' – the clever name he gave the bird, bringing together Alfred Jarry's 1896 satire on bourgeois self-satisfaction, *Ubu Roi*, with *hibou*, French for owl – was apt, literally, to bite the hands of those who fed him.

The bird had been found by Sima in a corner of the Musee d'Antibes, hobbled by a damaged claw. Picasso immediately bonded with the bird, and with Sima's help bandaged its leg back to health. According to Françoise Gilot, Ubu, back in Paris, installed in Picasso's aviary, didn't seem especially grateful. 'We were nice to him but he only glared at me. Any time we went into the kitchen, canaries chirped, pigeons cooed and turtle doves laughed, but the owl remained stolidly silent or at best snorted. He smelled awful and ate nothing but mice' – which she harvested from the reliably abundant population in the house's cellar. When the snorting occurred, Picasso would yell '*cochon, merde!*' but persisted nonetheless in trying to establish friendly relations with the glaring Ubu. There was something about the owl's refusal to ingratiate himself with his benefactors, of course, that Picasso admired. So despite the physical risks and discomforts, the clawing and scratching, the welts and the punctures, he persisted in coaxing the bird to sit in his hands and on his shiny head. 'Even then,' Gilot wrote in her memoir, 'he [Ubu] looked very unhappy.' Understandable; this was projection. The bad side of owls had been planted in the European mind along with the good, and Picasso the modernist revolutionary was nothing if not deeply engaged with classical antiquity. There was, on the one hand, the owl of Minerva that was a byword for wisdom and the many gifts of protection that would save Harry Potter. But at the same time, the nocturnal nature of owls has been thought of as sinister rather than benevolent.

FIG. 18
Pablo Picasso, *L'atelier (Les pigeons) (Velázquez)* (Studio [Pigeons] [Velázquez]), 1957. Oil on canvas, 129.5 cm × 96.5 cm. Museo Picasso, Barcelona.

FIG. 19
Michel Sima, *Pablo Picasso (Picasso and Owl, Antibes 1946)*, 1946. Gelatin silver print, 60.7 × 50.5 cm.

FIG. 20
Francisco de Goya, *El sueño de la razón produce monstruos* (The Sleep of Reason Produces Monsters), 1797–1799. Etching and aquatint on laid paper from *Los Caprichos*, plate 43, 306 × 201 cm, Museo Nacional del Prado, Madrid.

FIG. 21
Pablo Picasso, *Petite chouette* (Little Owl), 1951–1953.
Plaster, ceramic, metal and shellac, 33.5 × 22.5 × 19 cm. Kröller-Müller Museum, Otterlo.

Anyone looking at plate 43, initially intended as the title page of *Los Caprichos* of 1799, inscribed 'The Sleep of Reason Brings Forth Monsters', by Francisco Goya (1746–1828), would think of owls as the bringers of nightmares, madness and death (fig. 20). But for Picasso – embodied in Ubu's unchanging glare – Good Owl and Bad Owl were becoming one and the same, and they triggered in him, for a brief time, a whole parliament of the birds: ceramics, paintings, prints and a wittily suggestive little construction put together with found materials – a can lid to shape his head; nails for legs (fig. 21).

The effect of all this owl-mania (or perhaps the cause) was a wonderfully strange, increasingly ancient Egyptian-style indivisibility between artist and bird. Picasso said that many, including himself, had commented that he somewhat resembled an owl, and there came a time when the two entirely morphed together as 'Pablubu' (fig. 22).

The Neo-Cubist self-portrait, painted in 1952, Picasso called *The Owl of Death* and it was around this time, as he turned septuagenarian, that mortality began to occupy his still endlessly fertile mind, not least when Françoise Gilot had the temerity to leave him (fig. 23). But, as Picasso knew, he was not the only modernist to develop an avian alter ego, and one, moreover, that was the carrier of psychic disturbance to a much deeper and greater degree than Picasso's fly-by-night time of owls.

FIG. 22
Pablo Picasso, *Autoportrait en hibou* (Self-Portrait as an Owl), 1957. Pastel on paper, cut out over gelatin print, 534 × 370 mm. Whereabouts unknown.

FIG. 23
Pablo Picasso, *Le hibou de la mort* (The Owl of Death), 1952. Oil on canvas, 55 × 46 cm. Private collection.

FIG. 24
Max Ernst, *Loplop présente les membres du groupe surréaliste* (Loplop Introduces Members of the Surrealist Group), 1931. Cut-and-pasted gelatin silver prints, cut-and-pasted printed paper, pencil and pencil frottage on paper, 501 × 336 mm. The Museum of Modern Art, New York.

FIG. 25
Max Ernst, *L'Homme-oiseau et la femme masquée* (Bird Man and Masked Woman), 1934. Woodcut collage from *Une semaine de bonté* (A Week of Kindness), 20.5 × 15.5 cm. Museum Max Ernst Brühl des LVR.

Meet Loplop! Always self-conscious about his subconscious (an ardent reader of Freud), Max Ernst (1891–1976), one of Picasso's friends in Paris, had developed the hybrid bird as his alter ego, feathered avatar or daemon in the early 1930s, as a kind of master of Surrealist ceremonies, at once theatrical and feverishly creepy. Ernst had Loplop 'introduce' his circle – Paul Éluard, Salvador Dalí, Louis Aragon, Marcel Duchamp, André Breton and the rest – as if on a collective billboard, his beak peeping over its top (fig. 24). In his collage novel *Une semaine de bonté* (A Week of Kindness), Ernst has the figure with a bird's head and a human – well-tailored – body (rather like Horus in the form of a lanner falcon) pursue mostly incomprehensible adventures, one per each day of the week, through its pages (fig. 25).

But Ernst's compulsive identification with birds had begun long before that. When he was a child in Brühl, his pet cockatoo died at exactly the time his sister was born. One kind of bird ended the life of another and from that time on, the flight of birds did indeed turn into an interior vision of disaster. When, in 1897, he went down with a bad case of measles, the feverish boy hallucinated from the grooves in a mahogany panel opposite his sweaty bed disembodied bits of face – noses and ears – but also a bird. Those grooves reappear in 1924 in Ernst's *Two Children Are Threatened by a Nightingale*, as a trompe l'oeil solid frame beyond which lies the landscape of a dream (fig. 26). Little Max had watched his father paint landscapes; as his energetic mind worked its black magic he wanted to transform that illusory (because, art) world into a dreamscape of improbable terrors. So the painting has two entrances: our immersion into the work, and the work's tug into the unconscious. The nightingale? It flies remotely in the brilliant daylight that upends nature, and to all intents and purposes, innocently in the far distance. But it is obscurely terrifying enough that one of the 'children' (a girl very much drawn, in monochrome) brandishes a knife at it while another seems to have swooned away on the ground.

In 1936, the 18-year-old Leonora Carrington (1917–2011), multiply expelled from nun-run schools and in full teenage rebel mode, already writing poetry and short stories, and turning art student, received a book on Surrealism from her mother. Published in connection with the first International Surrealist Exhibition at the New Burlington Galleries in London, it included a plate of Ernst's painting as well as works from the usual suspects rounded up in Ernst's *Loplop*. As rooted to the spot – as anyone with eyes to use would be by Ernst's tour de force of cerebral-visual-tactile (for there was a real doorbell applied to it) – as she was, the appearance of the actual artist, twice her age but very good-looking with a striking nose that is impossible not to characterise as beaky, at a Hampstead dinner party given by Ursula and Ernö Goldfinger a year later, brought on, in short order, a massive psycho-erotic epiphany.

They went for it. Ernst left his wife. The couple moved to Paris just in time for the coming of war. In 1938, they moved south to St Martin d'Ardèche where they made sculptures of animals and, of course, birds. When war broke out, Ernst was arrested twice; first by the French for being an enemy alien, and then after spring 1940 by the Germans for being a 'degenerate artist'. In mortal danger, in December 1940 Ernst travelled to Marseille to stay with Varian Fry who specialised in the exit of writers, painters and musicians. The following year, Peggy Guggenheim, who had bought some of Ernst's work, arrived in Marseille, where she began to acquire him in person. Through Fry, Ernst secured a precious visa for a move to the United States and sailed from Lisbon with Guggenheim.

FIG. 26

Max Ernst, *Deux Enfants sont menacés par un rossignol* (Two Children are Threatened by a Nightingale), 1924.
Oil with painted wood elements and cut-and-pasted printed paper on wood with wood frame, 57.1 × 69.8 × 11.4 cm.
The Museum of Modern Art, New York.

In Spain, Carrington was so unhinged by misery that she was, catastrophically, admitted to an asylum in Santander for the mentally disordered where she was subjected to the usual, atrocious shock therapy, and a heavy prescription of chemical tranquillisers. In New York, Max Ernst, married to Peggy Guggenheim, was treated as a visionary lord of Surrealism.

Instructed to move to South Africa by her father, Leonora escaped her guardian in Lisbon where she sought out the Mexican poet Renato Leduc to whom she had been introduced by – of course – Pablo Picasso. Helpfully, Leduc proposed a marriage of convenience and was connected enough with the Mexican embassy to make their emigration possible. The rest of Carrington's life remained, happily, in Mexico City. She died at the age of 94.

In 1967, 30 years after she had met Max Ernst, Leonora did a gouache of an enormous, stately-portly bird that she named *Señor Ruiz, el Ruiseñor* (meaning nightingale) (fig. 27). She had never forgotten both the passion and misery the older artist had inflicted on her; and certainly not the portrait she had made at the height of their love affair, with His Beakiness covered in red feathers. This time, Ernst appears, unmistakeably, *inside* the bird-man, in monogram, as if in a photo of a prisoner looking out of his cell, his mouth opened in an 'O' suggesting a sound that was the opposite of the liquid beauty of nightingales. Perhaps he is now revealed as the kind of 'threatening' nightingale that in 1936 had drawn Leonora's intense, ultimately disastrous infatuation. Which would make this version of Ernst a prisoner of himself, perhaps. That would be very Leonora. But also Max to the max. In one of Carrington's magically gleaming fables – *The Seventh Horse* – a somewhat grouchy bird appears as a narrator, master of the plot, a role that Loplop enjoyed playing. The bird is described as fat, which, as far as I know, Max Ernst never was, and I very much doubt is a common trait of even the best-fed nightingales. But Carrington's *Señor Ruiz, el Ruiseñor* feathered in exactly the all-over style she had painted him in 1939, is grandiose in his corpulence (and a little mean above the neck), which would be, all things considered, an entirely understandable act of revenge.

FIG. 27 (Cat. 55, p. 155) Leonora Carrington, *Señor Ruiz, el Ruiseñor* (Señor Ruiz, the Nightingale), 1967. Gouache, c. 104 × 71 cm. Collection Betty and Homero Aridjis, Mexico.

But look, here is another bright-eyed goldfinch at the head of a line of fellow birds: robin, woodpecker, hoopoe, kingfisher and, lagging a little way behind, as they tend to do, a fine duck. Hieronymus Bosch (c. 1450–1516), who painted them, it is thought, between 1490 and 1510, has made them all, in comparison with the tiny humans who swarm his theme park of (mostly) fun, ENORMOUS (fig. 28). It is this absolute indifference to any and all rules of art, especially those laid down by Alberti a half century earlier, and including the goal of likeness that makes Bosch's goldfinch the polar opposite of Fabritius's perfectly rendered bird. Although the triptych was self-evidently not intended for a church, emblem hunters have spared no effort in decoding the symbolic associations (good luck with the hoopoe) and having to have the blood-splashed goldfinch represent 'Christianity'. Decoded, Bosch's fantastic scene, labelled *The Garden of Earthly Delights* on its acquisition by the Museo Prado in 1943, becomes a scene of vice, punished accordingly by the right-hand panel depicting Hell, scored to very rough music. It is now certain that the patron who commissioned the triptych was the rich Count of Nassau, Hendrik III, and Hans Belting has argued, most likely as the kind of intellectual puzzle-game that courts such as his could afford. In a bigger swerve Belting also believes that the central panel is actually an exercise in counter-Biblical anti-determinism: a vision of what paradise might have been had not the fatal bite been taken and the Fall ensued.

Possibly. And certainly more likely than an unequivocally offered denunciation of lechery. The giant goldfinch seems to be enjoying role-reversal. Instead of a captivity spent amusing humans, the man-lings, monochrome like the unformed universe Bosch painted on the front of the triptych's panels, are, while knee deep in water, entertaining the big bird dangling the blackberry just out of reach of their mouths. Those mouths are wide agape, exactly like the naked, blind, insatiably greedy hatchlings in a nest. This is fun – but not for the human chicks. There are other signs that give one pause in seeing the big scene as a paradisial orgy unburdened by the guilt of original sin. Close to the goldfinch's back a gloomy man-ling holds his hands over his ears. More usefully for Belting's argument of an Unfallen world, a figure identical to the Adam in the left panel, holds, or attempts to hold, Eve back from jumbo fruit. Taken altogether, the scene, despite a frolicsome pond for the girls and some interracial action, has an air of solemnity

FIG. 28
Hieronymus Bosch, *The Garden of Earthly Delights* (detail), c. 1490–1500. Oil on panel, 185.8 × 172.5 cm. Museo Nacional del Prado, Madrid.

hanging over the bare-bummed huddles and circular cavalcades like a screen orgy that knows it is running out of steam and is now following directions lest it grind to a halt.

If the sexual ornithology of Bosch's triptych remains a puzzle – as he may well have intended it to be – the same can't be said of the most famous story of intra-species sex. A brief episode in Ovid's *Metamorphoses* relates how Leda, the Queen of Sparta, was ravished by Jupiter, disguised as a swan. Thereafter, variations abound. Some have Leda lying with her husband the king that same night, so that she lays two giant eggs, one for each bedfellow. The hatched progeny usually include Helen, whose beauty brought ruin to Troy; some have Clytemnestra, who in murdering her husband Agammemnon set off the calamities visiting the house of Atreus. In other versions, the twins Castor and Pollux, the founders of the city of Rome, also emerge from an egg laid by Leda.

Images of the strange story occur early and often, all of them wrestling with the compositional problem of how to depict a bird coupling with a woman, even granting the suspension of disbelief accorded to Ovidian myths, with any anatomical credibility. Enterprising potters in classical antiquity, especially those catering to the broad indecency market, like the maker of a late 2nd–early 3rd century Roman terracotta oil lamp (given in 1917 to the Metropolitan Museum in New York by J.P. Morgan, no less), rose, or, rather, descended, to the challenge, Leda bends her knees to accommodate the bird, with a helpful assist from a rear-end cupid (fig. 29).

FIG. 29
Lamp fragment, Roman, late 2nd–early 3rd century. Terracotta, 7.15 cm high. The Metropolitan Museum of Art, New York.

But when the subject became popular again, early in the sixteenth century, and artists of the first rank including both Michelangelo (1475–1564) and Leonardo da Vinci (1452–1519) were commissioned by court patrons to paint the same subject, obligations of decorum arose. Both paintings were lost after they ended up in France, but both were copied by enough contemporaries to make clear very different approaches to solving the formal anatomical problem. A very beautiful Leonardo study drawing survives at Chatsworth in which Leda stands on her right leg while the swan does nothing more, but nothing less, than stretch up to nuzzle her ear with his beak. As in almost all versions of the story, most teasingly in a perfectly economic (or possibly ironic) Raphael drawing after Leonardo, Leda, her body lightly torqued, the smile very Mona Lisa, sets her hands on the long, thick neck of the swan, who, beak slightly opened, seems not unhappy to receive the caress (fig. 30).

FIG. 30
Raphael Sanzio, *Leda and the Swan*, c. 1507. Pen and ink over black chalk underdrawing, 310 × 192 mm. Royal Collection Trust, London.

Risky though the subject was, the Leda-swan story was popular enough for artists much further downmarket to give it a try. The most accomplished may have been the printmaker Giovanni Battista Palumba (n.d.), also known, given his name as well as his tastes, as Master of the Bird, signing his plates with a dove. One of the first graphic artists to produce independently authored prints, his swan wears a sinister expression, reminiscent of the serpent in Eden, as he curls round Leda's neck for a round of beaky osculation, while she clasps his body tightly between her thighs, the action echoed in the entwinings of vines about the surrounding trees. Premonitions of the Fall, all too obviously, are everywhere (fig. 31).

As one might expect, Michelangelo's version, a painting in egg tempera, known only from copies, and an engraving by the Dutch printmaker and publisher Cornelis Bos, some time between 1532 and 1555, is the one that comes closest to solving the problem of visual plausibility, by having Leda recline, her head lowered to meet the gentle kiss as the swan settles between her muscular legs, his head contentedly resting on her breast (fig. 33). To achieve the union of emotional intensity and physical grace - no easy thing given the absurdity of the myth - Michelangelo repurposed the recumbent allegorical sculpture of Night (itself inspired by classical reliefs) he had made for the Medici tombs in Florence. That figure's breasts and muscular thighs are transposed to Leda, but her head, documented in a glorious study drawing, now in Budapest, was slightly lowered to meet the upward-tilted beak of the amorous bird (fig. 32). Somehow, through an interpretative leap characteristic of his psychological inventiveness, the moment feels post- not pre-coital. For once, the embrace of skin and feathers is made to seem something akin to a tender communion rather than the indulgence of a pet bird.

FIG. 31
Giovanni Battista Palumba, reworked by Nicoletto da Modena, *Leda and the Swan Set in a Landscape*, 1500–1510. Partly hand-coloured engraving, 143 × 98 mm. The Metropolitan Museum of Art, New York.

The painting had been commissioned by Alfonso d'Este, Duke of Ferrara, when Michelangelo was inspecting the formidable fortifications of that city on behalf of the government of Florence. But the ducal representative who came to receive the work from the artist insisted on looking it over before payment. His judgement was that it was 'a little thing', implying that there might be a money issue. None of this, especially the presumptuous dismissal of the work, went down well with Michelangelo, who withdrew it and gave to his pupil Antonio Mini, who took it to France where it was acquired by King Francois I. When Cassiano dal Pozzo, secretary to cardinals and an art connoisseur, saw it at Fontainebleau in 1625, he was unmoved, while conceding it was 'finely done'. It seems likely, then, that its notorious reputation not only made beholders begrudge any admiration but might actually have doomed the painting.

A royal inventory of 1691 confirms that Anne of Austria, the queen of Louis XIII, ordered its destruction, along with a drawing 'earmarked to be burned'. Another drawing, once thought to be the cartoon for the tempera painting, ended up in the Royal Academy Schools in London in the eighteenth century where it was used for teaching. Predictably, in 1877, two Fellows of the Academy urged its removal on grounds that it was morally corrupting the students. Just as well, then, that outraged Victorian critics are unlikely to have seen the forthrightly pornographic painting attributed (not implausibly) to François Boucher, featuring the swan in an attitude of exploratory 'cunnibeccus'; just the kind of thing that appealed to the bird-fancying Louis XV.

Modernism did not dispense with Ovid's story; the rough force of one of W.B. Yeats's greatest poems wired together the violence of the ravishing with the historical catastrophes it engendered:

A sudden blow, the great wings beating still
Above the staggering girl, her thighs caressed
By the dark webs, her nape caught in his bill
He holds her helpless breast upon his breast.

FIG. 32
Michelangelo Buonarroti, *Studies of a Head*, c. 1530. Red chalk on paper, 355 × 269 mm. Szépművészeti Múzeum, Budapest.

FIG. 33 (Cat. 52, pp. 150-151)
Cornelis Bos after Michelangelo Buonarotti, *Leda and the Swan*, c. 1544–1545. Engraving, 302 × 410 mm. Rijksmuseum, Amsterdam.

FIG. 34
Cy Twombly, *Leda and the Swan*, 1962. Oil, pencil and crayon on canvas, 190.5 × 200 cm. The Museum of Modern Art, New York.

In the visual arts, it needed the implosive abstraction of Cy Twombly (1928–2011), living in Rome, his creative imagination nourished by immersion in the violent epics of antiquity, to render Yeats's 'shudder in the loins': the orgasmic throes of queen and bird, light years away from Michelangelo's serene coupling (fig. 34). Instead, Trombly's thrashing, haywire lines, with their graffiti hearts enact Yeats's poem:

> ...shudder in the loins engenders there
> The broken wall, the burning roof and tower
> And Agammemnon dead.

A fascination with the touch of swan down on human skin stuck in the mind of popular culture even when the rich source of the intimacy had been long forgotten. In 1935, Travis Banton, who had designed Marlene Dietrich's costumes for all her Joseph von Sternberg movies, dreamed up a number for a fancy, much photographed Hollywood dress party (fig. 36). Some 66 years later, with no nods to Leda, Michelangelo or Marlene Dietrich, Bjork wore a short, fully ruffled version of the swan dress, designed by Marjan Pejoski, to the 2001 Oscars ceremony (fig. 35). In case there was any confusion she laid six large ostrich eggs on the red carpet as the cameras were flashing. Taken as peak Bjork, a tour de force of kitsch, the swan dress was ridiculed by a press with no memory of the Dietrich costume, much less Ovid; one critic drily claiming that the swan had still been alive during rehearsals. Taken aback by the derision, Bjork was reduced to pleading 'it's just a dress.'

Which, of course, it never is. But Bjork's temporary discomfort is understandable. For centuries, plumage had been made available to enhance human display that was so often outshone by the most colourful of birds. To make the iridescent pins securing the very broad-brimmed hats in fashion in the late nineteenth and early twentieth century, entire, tiny hummingbirds were killed and decoratively impaled. In the second half of the nineteenth century, no funeral of the grand was complete without black ostrich plumes ornamenting black horses pulling the black carriage-hearse. But the demand of living fashion for ostrich feathers became so overwhelming that an entire industry in South Africa arose to supply it. Prior to that

FIG. 35
Jeffrey Mayer, *The 73rd Annual Academy Awards – Arrivals. Björk*, 2001. Colour photograph. WireImage.

FIG. 36
John Springer, *Actress Marlene Dietrich Dressed in Feathers*, 1935. Gelatin silver print, 31.7 × 25.6 cm. John Springer Collection, Iowa.

FIG. 37 (Cat. 28, p. 103)
Iris van Herpen, 'Idolomantis', *Roots of Rebirth Collection*, look 17, 2021. Duchess fabric, organza, mylar foil, cotton. Atelier Iris van Herpen, Amsterdam.

period, mounted ostrich hunters, matching the birds' legendary speed, had chased and killed the birds, the plumes being exported from North African ports to Europe. But this was far too haphazard to meet European and American demand. Breeding farms were established in South Africa from the mid-1800s, but they too were handicapped by the birds' uncanny reaction to their captivity, destroying eggs before they could be hatched. Accordingly, incubators were invented to ensure reliable hatching and the industry, if not the birds, took off, becoming by the turn of the century the fourth largest exporter from the region after, gold, diamonds and wool. Inevitably, oversupply crashed the market; prices collapsed and farms reverted to sheep.

In July 2018, the Dutch designer, Iris van Herpen (b. 1984) who trained as a classical ballet dancer, showed a collection (at Versailles, where engravings of the festivals of Louis XIV feature actor-dancers in spectacularly feathered costumes) of dresses that were, in effect, on the side of the birds, embodying not just imitative wonder at the biological marvel of feathered flight, but scientific analysis of its kinetic motion. Van Herpen's *Syntopia* show, orchestrated with a light display of moving glass tubes by Studio Drift, went as far as possible, given that the models were still grounded by their walking legs, to represent the motions of bird flight as if slowed by time-lapse vision. And in some cases, the transparent silk organza, laser-cut and layered like avian feathers, patterned according to the beats and movements of wings, and fluidly attached to the body, did actually manage to make the human disappear within an illusion of flight (fig. 37). All of the minute mathematical and anatomical calculations and calibrations that went into producing these effects were meant, for the first time in fashion, at any rate, to engineer a vision of bird vitality rather than mortality. The bird so created is a bird of Van Herpen's creative imagination, to be sure, but of that too Leonardo would surely have approved.

The approximation of avian and human experience, capable of registering bird life rather than frozen, ornamental death, seems right for a time when the entirety of nature on planet Earth is at hazard, and bird populations are in steep decline, whether through viral epidemics such as H5NI (aka bird flu) or the destruction of forest habitat. Van Herpen achieves this through the most technologically sophisticated means.

FIG. 38
Tracey Emin, *Self-Portrait as a Small Bird*, 2002. Soft-ground etching on thick wove paper, 280 × 320 mm. Oliver Clatworthy, London/ Los Angeles.

The interdependence of human and bird, especially with its fragile vulnerability, has also been personalised, most affectingly, by Tracey Emin (b. 1963), using the simplest and most traditional materials. Her *Self-Portrait as a Small Bird*, a soft-ground etching made in 2002, would have surprised only those who still saw Emin as a visual (and vocal) noise-maker, exclusively invested in confessional autobiography (fig. 38). The etching too is of a piece with personal declaration, but it has lost its clamour and replaced it with a little nightingale on a blossoming twig, drawn with a wavering line that makes the bird look tentative and fragile as a chick with wings that might, or might not, open. Emin, who took ornithology classes at school, has been sketching birds on and off for decades. But her own vulnerable side has led her naturally to identify not with the grandiose heraldry of the powerful – eagles, falcons and other raptors – but with the little birds of streets, parks and backyards – the underrated songsters of the urban grind. In 2005, she installed her first public work of art in front of Liverpool Cathedral's Oratory and called it, ironically, *Roman Standard*, replacing the eagle of the legions with a sparrow atop a four-metre bronze pole. The bird could only be seen from the side, disappearing when viewed from the front – and vanishing altogether when it was twice stolen, but, as if its very modesty carried a reproach to its thieves, twice returned. This was, for me at any rate, a wonderful reproach to the bombastic monumentalism of most public sculpture that demands respect from pedestrians (who barely notice the horsemen on plinths). In 2018, Emin continued in this strain in Sydney, installing 60 or so bronze birds on city sites – roofs, bus stops and the like – where they might easily be mistaken for living sparrows and encourage passers-by to stop and make a connection by touching them.

FIG. 39 (Cat. 53, pp. 152–153)
Tracey Emin, *You Saved Me*, 2014. Bronze, 31.5 × 51 × 34 cm. Studio Tracey Emin, courtesy White Cube Gallery, London.

Emin's recent battles with a very aggressive cancer have only strengthened her feeling that birds are, as she put it, 'angels on this earth' and that the fates of humanity and bird-life are interdependent. This elemental reciprocity was something Rachel Carson (1907–1964) wanted the world to understand when she wrote her fable of the *Silent Spring*, the poisoning that began, but would not end, with the disappearance of songbirds due to the softening of eggshells from the use of the insecticide DDT. Carson too was going through a battle with cancer when she wrote it in 1962.

You Saved Me is one of those declaratory titles Tracey Emin has used before, but when given to one of her small bronzes of a bird in flight with a human body flung over its back, the thanks are given to birds not men (fig. 39). For at this environmental tipping point in history, our own survival is, in some elemental way, conditional on theirs.

FIG. 40 (Cat. 34, pp. 116–117) Jan van IJken, *The Art of Flying*, 2015. HD video, black & white, 6 min 52 sec. Jan van IJken, Beesd.

Ten years ago, my wife and I were walking along a street in Rome's Trastevere district. The following morning I was due to receive a literary prize from the Accademia dei Lincei, founded in the time of, and including as a fellow, Galileo Galilei. So I was feeling pleased with myself. It was a mild autumn evening, the light gently closing in, when something overhead caught our eyes; something that, in a matter of seconds, corrected any unmerited sense of self-importance. High in the sky, thousands of birds, tens of thousands of them, perhaps hundreds of thousands, were wheeling and soaring, swooping, diving, rising up again, flying in one direction then turning and changing direction, a thick ribbon that unwound then coiled back up again or upended itself, so that we seemed to see, simultaneously, both sides of that avian helix. It was immediately obvious that there was nothing random in their movement; it was rather as though, choreographed, they were moving to an already-designed, patterning performance, the repeated, then varied, movements akin to a baroque fugue (fig. 40).

Italo Calvino, who witnessed this spectacle when he was living in Rome in the 1960s, has a lovely passage in his novella *Mr. Palomar*, when the protagonist compares a murmuration, in its alternating thickenings and separations, to the endless morphings of clouds, columns of smoke or jets of water. The experience is so hypnotically enfolding that at times Mr Palomar feels himself part of the great warp and weft of the birds. For some moments that was the way I felt too, that the ribbon formed by the immense murmuration wound round us too, tying together the arc of their lives with ours. Or so I wished it were the case, so that the most commonplace of birds were nonetheless deliverers of an ecstatic and profound miracle.

Due to a threat of war, in 1938 a red triangle was applied at the back of the panel, a mark reserved for irreplaceable masterpieces in the museum.

Cat. 1

Carel Fabritius, *The Goldfinch*, 1654. Oil on panel, 33.5 × 22.8 cm. Mauritshuis, The Hague, inv. no. 605.

Who Doesn't Want to be Friends with *The Goldfinch*?

Adrienne Quarles van Ufford

FIG. 1
Master of Catherine of Cleves, *Sts Cornelius and Cyprian*, p. 247, c. 1440. Parchment from *Hours of Catherine of Cleves*, 192 × 130 mm. The Morgan Library Museum, New York, MS M.917/945.

It is only a small painting, *The Goldfinch*, by the Delft artist Carel Fabritius (1622–1654), and it is so simple that you can take it in at a glance. Tethered by a fine chain around its leg, the bird looks at you. Or perhaps it would be better to say that it responds to your gaze. At once vulnerable and imperturbable. You know immediately that it can't get away. The picture aptly captures how humans hold on to birds they admire by robbing them of the very thing that characterises them, namely, their ability to fly (cat. 1, p. 45).

Although modest in size, only 33.5 by 22.8 cm, *The Goldfinch,* painted in 1654, has long enjoyed the admiration of countless viewers. The work is treasured for the fabulous way in which Fabritius painted it. The bird's posture, with its tilted head, beady eyes and colourfulness – note the strip of vivid yellow feathers on its wing and its red face – make it seem as if you were looking at a real (pet) animal.[1] With its feet gripping a bar, it sits in a well-lit spot, its body and the feeder casting a dark shadow on a damaged area of plaster on the wall behind it. All kinds of questions arise as a matter of course. Does the bird feel lonely? What is it like to live a constrained life? That is also part of the appeal. This masterpiece summarises how we as humans relate to birds in general. Admired for its colourful feathers, its song, its sense of community and its ingenuity, but imprisoned, imitated and, out of love for its company, kept captive for precisely these same reasons.

Did a real bird serve as a model for it? Fabritius was probably able to study a goldfinch up close, like the one he painted here. He probably didn't have to go into the woods to do so, since in the seventeenth century it was quite common to keep everyday birds at home, those we are still familiar with from our gardens, woods and hedges. Goldfinches, bullfinches, sparrows, larks and greenfinches were available for little money. Canaries or exotic parrots were far more expensive. They were mainly sold at the market.[2]

FIG. 2 (Cat. 35, p. 119) Anonymous, Glass pane with a chained goldfinch in front of a birdhouse, Netherlandish, c. 1650–1675. Grisaille paint on glass, 11.6 × 8.4 cm. Rijksmuseum, Amsterdam.

Goldfinches, in particular, were popular because they are eager to learn and it is easy to teach them tricks. A painted glass pane in the collection of the Rijksmuseum in Amsterdam shows the trick that gave the bird its nickname in Dutch, namely *puttertje*. Using a thimble-sized bucket attached to a string, the goldfinch could draw (*putten*) its own drinking water from a glass or bowl below it; therefore a *puttertje* (little *putter*) refers to something that draws water (fig. 2). This age-old domestic attraction was depicted as early as around 1440 in the *Hours of Catherine of Cleves*, in which a chained bird flies towards a thimble-sized bucket hanging from its open cage, which is shaped like a real house (fig. 1).[3]

This was not the only trick goldfinches could learn. The bird could open its own feeder or draw a cart full of seeds along a narrow plank using a pulley. The seventeenth-century poet Jacob Steendam (1616–1672/73) neatly captured its character. In his poetry collection *Den distelvink* (The goldfinch), he compared budding love to the little bird, from the moment it crawled, hoarse and awkward, out of its shell to the moment it was an attractive songbird. Steendam concluded: 'It is a nice animal, which rarely sits idle: It gets its own food and can draw its own drinks.'[4]

Humans have been keeping these birds for a long time. Even the Romans were fond of them: the famous writer Pliny the Elder (23/24–79) mentions them in his writings on account of their agility.[5]

For its part, Fabritius's goldfinch seems to be sitting still. Nothing in the picture tells us that this bird was very popular, not only for the tricks it could perform, but also for its clear, cheerful song. Males especially make themselves heard, even in captivity. And yet their natural high-pitched whistling, with its rapidly alternating range and variations, wasn't enough for every enthusiast. Goldfinches could learn religious or popular songs if you repeated them long enough using a whistle at the right pitch. Bird traders and animal owners went to great lengths to achieve this; from the eighteenth century on, they even used a special instrument, a so-called 'canary organ' or serinette. This music box used a bellows to produce high-pitched whistling sounds from tiny organ pipes. A family portrait by William Hogarth (1697–1764) shows a boy cranking up such a hand organ for a caged goldfinch (fig. 3).[6] In this way, humans tried to involve the bird even more in their own world.

FIG. 3
William Hogarth, *The Graham Children*, 1742. Oil on canvas, 160.5 × 181 cm. The National Gallery, London.

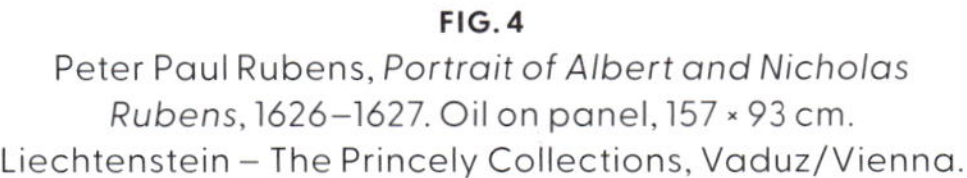

FIG. 4
Peter Paul Rubens, *Portrait of Albert and Nicholas Rubens*, 1626–1627. Oil on panel, 157 × 93 cm. Liechtenstein – The Princely Collections, Vaduz/Vienna.

FIG. 5
Raphael Sanzio, *Madonna of the Goldfinch*, before February 1506. Oil on panel, 107 × 77.2 cm. Galleria degli Uffizi, Florence.

It is no coincidence that the boy in Hogarth's painting is amusing himself with a goldfinch as this species had been a popular live toy since time immemorial. Peter Paul Rubens (1577–1640) also depicted his children with a goldfinch. In the beautiful *Portrait of Albert and Nicholas Rubens* (1626–1627), his boys are 13 and 9 years old. With furrowed brow, the younger of the two holds a crutch, a T-shaped stick with bells, to which the flying bird is attached with a string. The game of teaching a finch or sparrow to land on the crosspiece by pulling on the string had long been popular and remained so well into the nineteenth century (fig. 4).[7]

What the goldfinch itself thought about this is, of course, an open question, but for centuries humans regarded the bird as a friend of the family. The songbird also often appears with a more symbolic meaning, for example in a religious setting (fig. 5).[8]

In many paintings of Mary, the goldfinch is shown as a companion animal to the Christ Child, who sometimes almost squeezes the bird in his little fist. The meaning of its appearance in this context has little to do with child's play. According to a legend whose origin is difficult to trace, the goldfinch refers to the suffering that Jesus would face at the end of his life. This reading was inferred from the red spot on the bird's head, which was believed to be a drop of Christ's blood that stained the bird when, out of pity, it pecked a thorn out of Jesus's forehead. It was so common to see the Christ Child with a goldfinch that, even when the bird depicted is a greenfinch, great tit or an imaginary bird, it is still often referred to in the literature as a goldfinch.[9] This holds for *Virgin and Child Seated on a Turf Bench*, dating from around 1450 and coming from the studio of Dieric Bouts (c.1410/20–1475). The bird depicted is most likely an imaginary one: a green bird with a white neck and a black head does not exist in real life (fig. 6).[10] Regardless, the Christ Child himself does not seem bothered: he is thoroughly enjoying himself with the bird.

How did people get hold of these birds? Trapping finches and other songbirds had been widespread in the Netherlands since the Middle Ages, but it was not easy. Specialist bird- or finch-catchers used several methods, but the most lucrative involved bird traps during the autumn migration. Sons learned from their fathers how to set up traps on a 'finch route'. It was important to set the trap on a cleared patch of ground between bushes, loosening the soil and scattering seed and empty seed husks to keep the birds occupied for longer. Live decoy birds were kept in cages around the trapping area and tethered birds were set flying by pulling on the line attached to their legs: these attracted the wild birds, making it possible to ensnare entire migrating flocks. The catcher hid nearby and closed the trap – 'like two doors slamming shut' – by pulling on a cord laid flat on the ground or hidden in grooves on the side of the trap. With a bit of luck, 50 or even as many as 100 birds were caught each time (fig. 7).[11]

The series of drawings in the aforementioned *Hours of Catherine of Cleves* (fig. 1) shows how the decoy birds were prepared. Various methods were used to make them less frightened. They were also trained to sing continuously by gradually allowing light to re-enter their darkened cages. Less civilised methods were also used, however; it was very common to simply blind the decoy birds, which then sang even more.[12]

Most of the birds trapped using such decoys ended their lives in the pan or on the spit, but some were sold as pets. In the seventeenth century, and for centuries thereafter, many households had one or more cages containing songbirds, including goldfinches.[13]

We don't know to what extent Carel Fabritius, the painter of the famous *Goldfinch*, was aware of finch traps or the legend about the Christ Child. He probably would have been familiar with caged goldfinches, and the species, through the numerous sayings about birds in general and finches in particular. These often related to love and seduction. For example, Fabritius's contemporary, the poet Jacob Cats (1577–1660), often compared humans to birds, and finches specifically. He even shed light on relationships between the sexes by writing about a man who let himself be seduced by a woman at a place and time of her choosing, whereby he was unable to restrain himself and let himself be ensnared in her nets:

> I know that a certain woman, ignited by desire,
> named a place and set a time for you
> to catch you in her trap by cunning alone.
> You are like the finch that, driven by a great desire,
> falls from the sky to be caught by her.[14]

However, there is nothing to suggest that *The Goldfinch* should be associated with love. What is unusual about the work is precisely that; contrary to what was common practice in seventeenth-century painting, it provides no context. No story is depicted – there is just the little bird, which is portrayed somewhat from below. As a result, the painting will be shown to advantage when hung a little higher on the wall, just as one would a birdcage. The work is most likely a trompe l'oeil. Such works, which depict objects in such a way that it seems as if the viewer could grab hold of them, were particularly popular among art collectors of the time.

Research on the panel on which *The Goldfinch* is painted has confirmed this.[15] All the edges are painted white, which probably means it was originally displayed without a picture frame, and there have been several proposals about its original function. Was a shelf with a real, thimble-sized bucket and glass installed under the painted bird as a joke, so that the real world and the almost real bird formed a whole? Or did the panel serve as a door for a wall niche or even for a cabinet behind which a precious painting was located? Was it hung in a window frame to fool passers-by?[16]

FIG. 6 (Cat. 39, p. 132) Workshop of Dieric Bouts, *Virgin and Child Seated on a Turf Bench*, c. 1450. Oil on panel, 41.2 × 29.6 cm. Enschede, Rijksmuseum Twenthe.

FIG. 7
Philips Galle after Johannes Stradanus, *Finch Hunt with Net*, 1578.
Engraving, 199 × 283 mm. Museum Boijmans Van Beuningen, Rotterdam.

FIG. 8
Anonymous, Twenty-four nail tiles, Gouda, c. 1640–1660.
Majolica, 77.7 × 52 cm. Museum Boijmans Van Beuningen, Rotterdam.

FIG. 9
Anonymous, Plaque with birdcage, Delft, c. 1750–1800. Tin-glazed earthenware, 34.4 × 41.5 cm. Museum Arnhem.

FIG. 10
Carel Fabritius, *Young Man in a Fur Cap and a Cuirass (probably a Self-Portrait)*, 1654. Oil on canvas, 70.5 × 61.5 cm. The National Gallery, London.

Fabritius appears to have been not entirely alone in his successful but highly unusual attempt to conjure up a near-realistic housemate before the actual eye of the viewer. There is another variant of seventeenth-century trompe l'oeils featuring birds that has not been noticed before in this context. The creatures appear on rare ceramic tiles, made in Gouda and possibly also in Fabritius's hometown of Delft. A wide range of birds can be seen on these tiles, which in Dutch are called *spijkertegels* (nail tiles). Each bird appears to be sitting on a large nail that has been hammered into the wall. Whoever integrated such a tile into their kitchen, for example, had the pleasure of owning an almost real pet. In one set of these tiles, dating from between 1640 and 1660, a goldfinch can be seen on the third tile from the left in the fourth row from the top. The tiles were made around the same time that Fabritius painted *The Goldfinch* (fig. 8).[17]

People were so keen to be in the company of birds, whether real or painted, that earthenware tablets featuring illusionistic birdcages were made in the eighteenth century; most of them feature a yellow canary, but goldfinches are also common. It seems that people want to have these birds close to them (fig. 9).[18]

One would like to know, of course, whether Carel Fabritius frequently painted this kind of trompe l'oeil. Unfortunately, only around twelve of his paintings are known to exist, none of which is a trompe l'oeil. The artist died young, in 1654, the year in which he painted *The Goldfinch*. He was only 32 (fig. 10).

Fabritius was one of around 500 people who died as the result of an explosion in a gunpowder store in Delft, which caused great devastation in the city. It is assumed that many of his paintings were destroyed at the same time. It is a small miracle that *The Goldfinch* survived – small dents in the surface indicate that the paint on the panel had not even hardened when the fatal explosion occurred.[19]

Fabritius was one of the most gifted pupils to study under Rembrandt (1606–1669), alongside Samuel van Hoogstraten (1627–1678), who would go on to become a prolific painter of trompe l'oeils. Rembrandt was working on illusionistic phenomena in his paintings when

Fabritius was present in his studio – first as a young pupil and then possibly as an assistant: from around 1635 to 1643 or even later.[20] The master gave his own unique twist to trompe-l'oeil 'trickery': for example, in *The Girl in a Picture Frame* (1641), he depicted the hands of a young woman in such a way that it seems as if she herself were holding the (painted) frame.[21]

After the Delft Explosion or 'Thunderclap', as the catastrophic event of 1654 came to be known, there followed a period of quiet regarding *The Goldfinch* that lasted two centuries.[22] Both Carel Fabritius himself and his small masterpiece fell into oblivion. But then the work began to attract attention again, first cautiously and then with increased enthusiasm. It was first shown in 1867 at an exhibition in Amsterdam organised by the artist association Arti et Amicitiae. In 1896, it was purchased by the Mauritshuis and immediately became a public favourite, its popularity fuelled by numerous articles in the media.

From the start, the bird was described as if it were a living creature. 'How characteristically and with a deep sense of the intimacy of nature is the expression of the head rendered, with its sparkling eye. So too the legs and the tender, fluffy little body,' said the Dutch newspaper *Het nieuws van den dag* on 16 March 1896. The artwork had been acquired just two weeks earlier on the orders of Abraham Bredius (1855–1946), director of the Mauritshuis, at an auction in the French capital. Bredius himself travelled by train to collect it. 'Just back from Paris – where I acquired the C. Fabritius 1654!', a clearly excited Bredius wrote to Frederik Obreen (1840–1896), director of the Rijksmuseum, on 29 February. He also mentioned the previous owner of the artwork.[23]

Such a provenance was considered a mark of quality. The Frenchman to whom he was referring, Théophile Thoré (1807–1869), was a highly regarded art critic and researcher who had obtained political asylum in Brussels, where he lived for years under the pseudonym William Bürger and published on seventeenth-century Dutch art. He was a great admirer of Johannes Vermeer (1632–1675) and, in his slipstream, of Fabritius, whom he considered to be Vermeer's teacher, although this later proved to be incorrect. Thoré travelled all over Europe to research these artists, but he also made unexpected discoveries closer to home. Indeed, it was in Brussels that he came across Fabritius's *Goldfinch* in the 1850s under a thick layer of dust, hidden amid the jumble in the attic of a friend, art collector Chevalier Joseph-Guillaume-Jean Camberlyn. For Thoré, it was love at first sight. He was reportedly allowed to take the work home temporarily, where he cleaned it and 'brought the little winged creature back to life'. In 1865, after Camberlyn's death, and after some insistence on his part, Thoré was gifted the work by a member of Camberlyn's family. He named it *Le chardonneret* (*The Goldfinch*) and cherished it as a treasure until his death.[24]

After the Maritshuis acquired *The Goldfinch*, the work's popularity was bolstered in other ways, some of them unexpected. For example, the year it was purchased, the aptly named photography firm Vinkenbos & Dewald (*vinkenbos* literally means 'forest of finches') released a professional photograph of the painting. An etching of the panel by the artist Philip Zilcken also helped to popularise it. The etching, which Zilcken had already exhibited with Arti et Amicitiae in Amsterdam in the autumn of 1896, was a success – and spread the love for *The Goldfinch* even further.

But the artwork only really achieved its star status after American author Donna Tartt used the bird as the starting point for her novel *The Goldfinch* (2013), which was made into a film in 2019. When the painting was displayed at The Frick Collection in New York in 2013/14, alongside other highlights from the Mauritshuis, it was one of the crowd-pullers, together with Vermeer's *Girl with a Pearl Earring*.[25] Some 200,000 visitors came to see it; people stood in long queues in the bitter cold for a ticket. In 2016, something similar happened at the Scottish National Gallery in Edinburgh, when the exhibition *The Goldfinch* attracted more than 88,000 visitors in the space of six weeks. Since then, it is no longer just art lovers, holidaymakers with children and absorbed museum visitors who pause in front of the artwork in the Mauritshuis, but also many members of reading clubs and film enthusiasts who come to see the legendary little bird. Literary authors from across the Western world, including Laura Cumming, Benjamin Moser, Donna Tartt and Joost Zwagerman, have all felt a strong attraction to the work.[26]

In descriptions of the piece, the bird is sometimes even given near human characteristics, as in *Thunderclap: A Memoir of Art and Life and Sudden Death,* Cumming's 2023 book. She writes: 'This bird has a specific force of personality, an air of solitude and sorrow, a living being looking out at another living being from its prison against the wall.' And even though the bird is made of paint and brushstrokes, perhaps it is precisely this humanisation that ultimately gives the goldfinch its ultimate freedom, as a thinking, feeling individual that transcends time and place.

1 The red paint used to render the head has faded slightly over the course of time. Noble et al. 2008, p. 150.
2 Matthey 2002, p. 278, 280.
3 Thóth-Ubbens 1969, p. 156.
4 Steendam 1649-1651, p. 1v.
5 Thóth-Ubbens 1969, p. 155; Friedmann 1946, p. 31, note 65.
6 See, e.g., *Canary Organ (Serinette)*, c. 1820. 16.8 × 27.5 × 19.5 cm. Museum Speelklok, Utrecht, inv. 0748. With thanks to Friedell ten Holt-Dekkers and Axel Schering from Museum Speelklok, Utrecht.
7 Matthey 2002, pp. 280–282.
8 For the appearance of the goldfinch in a different iconographic context, see, among others, Friedmann 1946, pp. 7–35; De Jongh 1967, p. 46, 49; Broos 1987, pp. 136–139; Matthey 2002, pp. 273–276; Van Suchtelen 2004, pp. 135–138 and references in notes 5–7.
9 Friedmann 1946, p. 1.
10 With thanks to Gerald Derksen, Vogelbescherming Nederland (Society for the Protection of Birds, Netherlands).
11 Chomel 1743, pp. 1250–1252; Matthey 2002, pp. 100–121.
12 Thóth-Ubbens 1969, p. 155; Matthey 2002, p. 61. Van Deursen 2009, p. 128.
13 Matthey 2002, pp. 261–268, 276–279. Capturing native birds has been prohibited in the Netherlands since the 1912 Bird Act.
14 Cats 1712, vol. 1, p. 543. Quoted in Matthey 2002, p. 306.
15 Boström 1950, pp. 81–83; Wadum 2004, pp. 24–30; Noble et al. 2008, pp. 146–155.
16 Brown 1981, pp. 47–48; Broos 1987, no. 24, pp. 138–139. For a summary of the possible options in the literature, see Van Suchtelen 2004, pp. 136–138; Stone-Ferrier 2016, pp. 1–32.
17 With thanks to Suzanne Lambooy, Kunstmuseum Den Haag. See https://www.boijmans.nl/en/collection/artworks/16191/twenty-four-bird-tiles, accessed on 18 August 2025. We ignore whether the above little pane (fig. 2) with the painted goldfinch can also be considered a trompe l'oeil. It is part of a series of painted panes featuring birds, but also flowers, which have been in the care of the Rijksmuseum since 1890. The fact that individual flowers are visible on some makes it less logical to interpret it as a trompe l'oeil. With thanks to Matthias Ubl, Rijksmuseum, Amsterdam.
18 With thanks to Suzanne Lambooy, Kunstmuseum Den Haag. See, e.g., Anonymous (Delft), *Plate with Birdcage Shape and Decoration*, 1760–1780. Tin-glazed earthenware, 27.4 × 30 cm. Kunstmuseum Den Haag (inv. 1059758); or Anonymous, *Plaque with Image of a Birdcage*, 18th or 19th century. Tin-glazed earthenware, 25.6 × 25.3 cm. Museum De Lakenhal, Leiden, inv. 8029.
19 Noble et al. 2008, p. 154.
20 Brown 1981, p. 17; The Hague/Schwerin 2004–2005a, p. 17; Seelig 2006, p. 97; Schatborn 2006, p. 137.
21 Rembrandt, *Girl in a Picture Frame*, 1641. Oil on panel, 105.5 × 76.3 cm. Royal Palace, Warsaw; Vienna 2025, pp. 153–176.
22 Van der Mark 2004, pp. 20–22.
23 Letter from Abraham Bredius to Frederik Obreen, 29 February 1896. Archief Mauritshuis, NL-HaMH_2.14.130_90_019. Martinet auction, Hôtel Drouot, Paris, 27 February 1896 (lot 16).
24 Suzman Jowell 2016, pp. 72–77; The Hague/Schwerin 2004–2005b, p. 138.
25 New York 2013.
26 Cumming 2023; Moser 2023; Tartt 2013; Zwagerman 2015, pp. 103–109.

Stilled Flight

Martine Gosselink

Eat or be eaten, hunt or be hunted. Things are no different in the avian world. We humans hunt birds and hunt with birds. The main reason for hunting birds has always been to obtain food. We also want to collect and mount birds, study them, use their feathers to embellish ourselves. We want to cage birds to look at them and listen to them. Do we bring birds into our homes because we'll never be able to enter theirs? Why do we hold captive living creatures that have been given the sky to soar in by nature?

The Valkhof Museum in Nijmegen houses an urn containing the bones of 28 song thrushes. Made of clay from the Ardennes, the urn served as a kind of tin can and was thrown away after use. It was found during the excavation of a latrine at a nearby Roman army camp dating from the first century. The song thrushes – considered a delicacy by the Romans – were probably caught in the Ardennes and then seasoned and preserved in the pot. It is likely that the soldiers threw away the urn and its contents because the meat had spoiled. Song thrushes, along with the remains of geese, ducks, pigeons, cranes, cormorants and long-eared owls, have repeatedly been found among archaeological offal throughout the Limes, the frontier regions of the Roman Empire. We know from Roman recipe books that they also ate cranes; they would sew their eyes shut, leading the birds to move less and fatten up more quickly.[1] Hunting methods included nets, bows and arrows, spears, slings, glue and traps. These methods are still used today; others have been added over time, such as firearms and poison. And there is another: the emptying of nests. The ninth-century Chinese poet Pi Rixiu wrote about deadly ascents in the Mountains of Long to take parrots from nests. The parrots were intended as a tribute to the emperor, who would then release the birds:

> The Mountains of Long – a thousand myriad fathoms:
> The parrots build their nests on the very peaks.
> Were all of their perils and hazards explored,
> These mountains would still not be comprehended.
> Doltish and dull-witted, these people of Long
> Climb and clamber as if ascending to heaven.
> Should they spy such a nest up in the void,
> They still will fight over it even as they fall.
> Of a hundred birds, they do not get one;
> But of each ten men, nine die in this pursuit.
> By Long Stream are the garrison recruits;
> The garrison recruits are not idle either:
> By mandate, they must take up the carved cages
> And go straight to the Front of the Gilded Terrace
> [the imperial palace].
> But this plumage is not of value to itself,
> This tongue does not speak for itself.
> To what end this slighting of human lives
> To offer up such trifles for play and pleasure?
> I have heard that an ancient king, a paragon,
> Let each of his costly birds go free:
> Yet now these people here of Long
> Must weep floods of tears each year.[2]

Hanging from a nail on a wall (cat. 7, p. 68), the dead partridge painted by Jan Baptist Weenix (1621–1659) would have been killed with a gun. Weenix – who trained the virtuoso bird painter Melchior d'Hondecoeter (1636–1695) (cat. 15, p. 82), intended his partridge as a trompe l'oeil, just like *The Goldfinch*. The spectator seems to see the bird dangling on the faded wall, tied up by one leg with a cord, the meat in the process of ageing (small game is best hung for a few days before cooking, so that the meat can grow tender and gain in flavour). Although the partridge is lifeless, its body possesses movement: that one outstretched wing, the theatrically dangling leg, the vivid shadow.

Does Weenix's partridge represent anything, besides being a symbol of hunting? Art historian Eddy de Jongh recognised signs of sexual arousal in seventeenth-century depictions of partridges. De Jongh came across a passage in a letter from Caspar Barlaeus to P.C. Hooft that confirms this symbolism. Barlaeus, who had just become a widower, was writing in response to a gift he had received from Hooft, namely a bunch of partridges: 'That you should send partridges to me of all people, a widower, is strange in every respect. It is the most lustful bird you send me, symbol and hieroglyph of Venus, the sight of which reminds me of the caresses that I, as a widower, must do without. What is this but whetting the appetite of a hungry man who doesn't have what he longs to eat? You should have sent a sad, deathlike night owl to a sad and beaten man: a desolate nightbird for a desolate man living on his own... Swans, pigeons, partridges, sparrows, these are birds for yourself, for they are dedicated to matrimony, in which one follows their example in terms of kissing, caressing, embracing and pleasure; but the birds for me are owls and bats and other birds of the night, accustomed to hooting and howling.'[3] In this context, Weenix's lifeless partridge could be interpreted as the end of desire or the death of a loved one.

Jan Weenix (1640–1719), son of Jan Baptist Weenix, also painted a dead bird, also hanging by a leg and with a wing spread open, but this bird is a swan (cat. 11, p. 72). Beyond that, there are not many similarities between the two still lifes: the partridge is all simplicity and austerity, while the swan is particularly sumptuous. The client could flaunt his social status with this showpiece, because only the elite were allowed to hunt swans. The large size of the picture is not very Dutch, but it's probably because the 75-year-old Weenix had just finished a series of colossal hunting still lifes for a castle in Düsseldorf, commissioned by the Elector Palatine.

Not everyone was allowed to hunt. In feudal times, both hunting grounds and game itself were classified according to rank and class. For centuries, hunting big game was

FIG. 1
Woman Engaged in Falconry. Miniature from *The Taymouth Hours*, fol. 74, c. 1325–1350. The British Library, London, Yates Thompson MS 13.

strictly reserved for the nobility, while the hunting rights for small game – rabbits, hares, ducks, pheasants, partridges, snipe and herons – were distributed among the other social classes. Even so, such rights were only granted under certain conditions. There was one exception: crows. Anyone could kill these birds, not only on account of the damage they caused to crops, but also because of their reputation: the black carrion bird was a bringer of misfortune and death.

For the nobility, hunting was primarily a pleasure, preferably carried out in the company of other noble families to strengthen mutual ties. After the hunt, dinners were organised in the woods. From the twelfth century onwards, women (fig. 1) also took an active part in hunting – mainly with birds of prey: falcons, hawks, sparrowhawks and buzzards – thereby opening up additional opportunities for courtly love.

The portrait of Robert Cheseman by Hans Holbein the Younger (1497/98–1543), shows a gyrfalcon trained by humans (cat. 12, p. 73). Cheseman seems comfortable with the falcon, whose eyes are covered with a leather hood to keep it calm. These kinds of hoods were sometimes inlaid with precious stones and decorated with the feathers of a bird of paradise; here, it has only been embellished with a dab of paint. A strap with a bell is attached to the bird's left leg, so that it, and its prey, can be found quickly. Cheseman is stroking the bird with his right hand while gripping the leg strap with his left hand. All in all, he seems ready for the hunt. Or is he? In England, falconry, the most noble form of hunting, was a royal privilege until 1792 – no doubt because the falcon is a mighty hunter (the peregrine falcon is the fastest animal in the world, with a diving speed of 390 kilometres per hour). For a long time, Cheseman – portrayed here at the age of forty-eight in 1533, as indicated by the Latin inscription – was thought to be depicted in his role as chief falconer to King Henry VIII. Talking of hunting or being hunted, it is worth noting that the painting was once part of England's royal art collection. After he was crowned king of England in 1689, William III took the painting from the English court to decorate his hunting palace Het Loo in Apeldoorn.

Various travel accounts shed light on how important falconry – including the falcons themselves – was to the nobility. Many European travellers marvelled at the large numbers of birds of prey owned by monarchs in Egypt and Turkey. For example, the fifteenth-century knight and traveler Bertrandon de la Broquière mentions that a lord in Karamania (Turkey) owned 2,000 hunting birds and 1,000 hunting dogs. Traveler Joos van Ghistele from the same period notes that a former sultan living in Alexandria employed as many as 50 men in the daily training and care of saker and peregrine falcons as well as gyrfalcons.[4] No less illustrative are the twelve Greenland gyrfalcons that formed part of the ransom paid by the Burgundian count Philip the Bold to the Turkish ruler Sultan Bayezid to secure the release of his son John. Later known as John the Fearless, he had been captured when his Crusader army was defeated in 1396. The sultan was a great amateur of falconry and is said to have accepted the gyrfalcons – then the most valuable hunting birds in the world – as a welcome addition to his collection, which was managed by hundreds of falconers.[5]

The falcon was also a prominent status symbol outside the Middle East and Europe, in China, Mongolia and North Africa. The first written account of falconry, dating from as early as 244, comes from Japan.[6] The place name 'Valkenswaard' in the Netherlands recalls the passion for falcons (*valken*) in the region. From the late Middle Ages until the French Revolution, Belgian falconers (often trained at Arendonk) worked at courts across Europe and as far away as Iceland. The Holy Roman Emperor Frederick II, depicted here with his falcon (fig. 2), was the author of the famous *De arte venandi cum avibus* – literally *The Art of Hunting with Birds*, commonly known as *The Art of Falconry* – around 1245. He identified bird species, wrote about how to care for birds of prey and carried out research, studying whether ostrich eggs could be hatched using the heat of the sun, for example. For centuries, *The Art of Falconry* was the most important handbook for falconers. Several copies of the book have been preserved; the image of Frederick II shown here comes from a parchment copy kept in the Vatican.

Wherever hawking took place, the close bond between the falcon and the owner was always of prime importance. Sometimes, the falconer and the bird seemed inseparable. There is a reason for that: birds of prey can't be tamed – they always remain wild – so it takes a lot of patience to gain their trust. Some, like owls, must be trained at a very young age; once the chick regards its handler as its biological parent, their relationship will flourish. The art then consists in the trainer knowing how to arouse the bird's hunting instinct when he wants to make use of it. After that, trainer and animal must stay together so that the bird remains accustomed to the trainer. Perhaps that is why there are several Indian miniatures of the eighteenth-century Mughal emperor Muhammad Shah with his falcon. For instance, the bird is present when the emperor receives his vizier, Mir Qamar-ud-din Khan Siddiqi, in a tent in a work from 1736 (cat. 3, p. 64). The vizier was one of the emperor's key confidants, and the two men shared a close bond. The emperor was desperately saddened when, twelve years after this meeting, the vizier was fatally struck by a cannonball during a military campaign against the Afghans. Muhammad Shah reportedly died of grief soon after.

Apart from the specifics of hunting, captured birds provided ample material for public entertainment. The most cruel games, now banned for decades, were played with these feathered animals. They were traded at bird markets and taken home as pets – because they were beautiful, for their song or simply for company. The image of a bird in a cage has great visual power and has been used as metaphor since time immemorial. Around 524, the Roman statesman and philosopher Boethius wrote his famous work *The Consolation of Philosophy*. He completed it in prison, awaiting execution for high treason against his former friend, King Theodoric the Great. In the following passage, he writes about birds in cages, the message being that every bird wants to be where it belongs, in nature:

> If the bird who sings so lustily upon the high tree-top, be caught and caged, men may minister to him with dainty care, may give him cups of liquid honey and feed him with all gentleness on plenteous food; yet if he fly to the roof of his cage and see the shady trees he loves, he spurns with his foot the food they have put before him; the woods are all his sorrow calls for, for the woods he sings with his sweet tones.... All things must find their own peculiar course again, and each rejoices in his own return. Not one can keep the order handed down to it, unless in some way it unites its rising to its end, and so makes firm, immutable, its own encircling course.

FIG. 2
Frederick II with his Falcon. Miniature from *De arte venandi cum avibus* (The Art of Falconry), fol. 1, late 13th century. Biblioteca Apostolica Vaticana, Vatican City, Pal. lat 1071.

This blue ceramic cage, made in Delft around 1800, (cat. 4, p. 65) is a rather distinguished version of a birdcage. It's so small – only 30 by 30 cm – that it is hard to imagine that it ever contained a living animal. It is painted in the cobalt blue so typical of Delftware. Small landscape scenes appear on all sides. On the left, a woman sits beside a man; an empty birdcage stands next to her, while a bird perches on her hand. In the seventeenth century, everyone knew that an empty birdcage meant that love had been consummated, with the cage representing the female genitals and the bird, whether it had flown away or not, virginity. Whether this meaning still held around 1800 is an open question.

Some 70 years later, this pendulum clock (cat. 2, p. 63) was created in the workshop of Blaise Bontems, a Parisian manufacturer of automatons. Museum Speelklok in Utrecht owns four automata by Bontems, and this giant clock – an impressive 94 cm tall – is one of them. The glass dome contains a miniature tree with mounted birds, a waterfall and a sailing ship. When the mechanism is wound up, a wonderful scene unfolds, accompanied by music and chirping. Bontems was interested in taxidermy (especially of birds) from an early age, and picked up the sounds he used for his mechanical songbirds during walks in the Forêt de Fontainebleau.

The clock's three birds are connected by virtually invisible wires. Two hummingbirds dash from one twig to another, drink from the waterfall and peck at food on the ground while the bird at the top spreads its wings. Water cascades down the waterfall (Bontems used a rotating crystal rod and a moving light reflector to imitate flowing water). At the same time, the machinery makes the ship appear to rock on the waves.

Nowadays, we tend to hunt birds because they pose a threat or cause problems for humans. For example, to prevent the spread of disease, such as bird flu, to avoid them colliding with aeroplanes, to stop them damaging crops or because they poop on cars. In the Netherlands, large numbers of geese are driven into traps before being gassed because of the problems they cause, including noise pollution, environmental damage and danger to traffic as well as their aggressive behaviour. This is only feasible in the moulting season, when they are unable to fly.

One of the most memorable moments in Dutch bird hunting history happened on 14 November 2005, when an unsuspecting sparrow flew into the Frisian Expo Centre, where 3.5 million dominoes had been set up for World Domino Day four days later; the idea was to break the world record by toppling 4.3 million dominoes with a single push. The (female) sparrow knocked something and caused 23,000 dominoes to fall prematurely. The decision was made to shoot her. The furore afterwards was enormous, ranging from threats against the shooter to a dedicated website for the bird with a book of condolences. The domino sparrow (cat. 5, p. 66) was eventually mounted, without the wing that had been shot off, and is on display at the Natural History Museum in Rotterdam.

Eat or be eaten, that's how this chapter began. And you can take that literally. On a Sunday afternoon in March 2018, a homeless man lit a campfire in the Haagse Bos, a large city forest in the Hague. On it, he roasted a heron, carefully plucked beforehand. While nibbling the legs, he was approached by police officers who had been alerted by the smoke; after all, open fires are not allowed in the Haagse Bos nature reserve. The officers took him away and discarded the gnawed legs. Rotterdam's Natural History Museum heard the remarkable story via local media and went to the police in search of the legs, which are now part of the museum's collection (cat. 8, p. 69).[7] The museum's staff christened the bird *Kluifrègâh* (knuckle heron) in view of its history. The grey heron (*Ardea cinerea*) has been a protected bird in the Netherlands since 1963, but the homeless man wasn't concerned by that. The heron probably died of natural causes, due to the freezing cold anyway. People didn't make a fuss about such matters in the past: according to museum ornithologist Karel Voous, Henry VIII of England held a grand banquet in 1532 in which no fewer than 440 herons were served to his guests.

This chapter is about how we humans hunt birds and prevent them from flying. The animals aren't so much under threat because we eat them, cage them or kill them for their feathers. Even our domestic cats, which regularly come home with dead birds, are not the biggest threat. It's the way we treat our planet. To name just a few issues: severe air pollution, oil in the sea, pesticides on crops, and microplastics in our habitat, which we share with birds. Who does not remember the dying swan from Greenpeace's 1997 campaign *No Time to Waste* (cat. 9, p. 70)? Dancer Sabine Chaland becomes entangled in a mass of oil while performing *The Dying Swan* to music by Saint-Saëns, and dies. This particular campaign opposed oil drilling in the Arctic, which threatened the region's fragile ecosystem.

1 Boussauw 2024, p. 94.
2 Idema 2025, p. 11.
3 De Jongh 1967, p. 28.
4 Martens 2010.
5 Ibid.
6 Boëthius 2009.
7 *Natuurhistorisch Museum Rotterdam* n.d.

Cat. 2

Blaise Bontems, Clock with musical movement and automata, c. 1870.
Taxidermy, wood, glass, metal, 94 × 60 × 34 cm. Museum Speelklok, Utrecht, inv. no. 0049.

< Detail of Blaise Bontems's clock.

Cat. 3

Anonymous, *Muhammad Shah Receives Qamar-ud-din Khan*, 1736. Gouache, gold and opaque paint with brush, 325 × 241 mm. Rijksmuseum, Amsterdam, inv. no. RP-T-1973-56.

Cat. 4

Plateelbakkerij De Grieksche A, owner Pieter Jansz. van Marksveld, *Birdcage*, 1796–1811; and detail of the left side. Tin-glazed earthenware (faience) painted in cobalt blue, 34.5 × 31.2 × 14.7 cm. Kunstmuseum The Hague, inv. no. 0400704.

Cat. 5

Dominomus (Domino Sparrow), 2005/2015.
17 × 11 × 11 cm. Natural History Museum Rotterdam,
inv. no. NMR 9989-02269.

Cat. 6

John James Audubon, *American Flamingo*,
1827–1838. Hand-coloured aquatint
from *The Birds of America*, vol. 5, plate 432.
Teylers Museum, Haarlem, inv. no. WBW 08140.

Cat. 7

Jan Baptist Weenix, *Dead Partridge, Hanging from a Nail*, c. 1650–1652. Oil on canvas, 50.6 × 43.5 cm. Mauritshuis, The Hague, on long-term loan from the Friends of the Mauritshuis Foundation, since 1960, inv. no. 940.

Cat. 8

Kluifrègâh, 2018. *Ardea cinerea* (grey heron), adult, two legs, gnawed. Natural History Museum Rotterdam, inv. no. NMR 9989-05889.

Cat. 9

'Dying swan' from the Greenpeace campaign *No Time to Waste*, 1997. Dancer Sabine Chaland; director Trevor Wrenn.

Cat. 10

Rembrandt, *Still Life with Peacocks*, c. 1639. Oil on canvas, 145 × 135.5 cm. Rijksmuseum, Amsterdam, inv. no. SK-A-3981.

Rembrand

Cat. 11

Jan Weenix, *Dead Swan*, 1716.
Oil on canvas, 173 × 154 cm. Museum Boijmans Van Beuningen, Rotterdam, inv. no. 1962.

Cat. 12

Hans Holbein the Younger, *Portrait of Robert Cheseman (1485–1547)*, 1533. Oil on panel, 58.8 × 62.8 cm. Mauritshuis, The Hague, inv. no. 276.

The Fate of the Flightless

Martine Gosselink

Which came first, the chicken or the egg? The chicken, of course, or have you ever seen an egg lay a chicken? Just kidding, the correct answer is both at the same time. The chicken species gradually evolved out of other organisms that came from eggs; think of the dinosaurs and the first bird, *Archaeopteryx*, some 150 million years ago. In any case, a fertilised egg produces a chick. We humans associate chicks not only with spring, but also with cuteness overload. Aren't they just so sweet, those little yellow balls of fluff chirruping away as they scratch around on their wobbly legs?

Melchior d'Hondecoeter (1636–1695), the renowned bird painter, knew how to capture them on canvas like no other. His study of seven chicks in different poses (cat. 15, p. 82) helped him to grow as an artist: they served as models for countless bird paintings he went on to create. He reused these seven young fowls in many other paintings: lying down, trying to fly or pecking grain on the ground. No other artist of his time – he was one of the first to choose our feathered friends as his main subject – painted as many different birds as D'Hondecoeter: pigeons, swallows, magpies, chickens, cocks and geese, but also exotic birds including peacocks, pelicans, cranes, flamingos and cassowaries, which he let flap about or had pose on baroque walls in park-like surroundings. His models were often the most beautiful and colourful males. Incidentally, he hardly ever painted eggs.

The egg has been a symbol of spring and fertility long before Christianity. There's a reason that Constantin Brancusi (1876–1957) named his bronze egg from 1924 *The Beginning of the World* (fig. 1). With the rise of the Christian Church, priests found it difficult to stamp out all kinds of local rituals which they considered pagan. They therefore decided to integrate these old traditions into the emerging Christian customs. This included the egg as a symbol of new life. Eating eggs and meat was forbidden during Lent, the period preceding Easter. But then, at Easter, when the cycle of death (Christ's crucifixion) and life (his resurrection) was commemorated, you were allowed to eat eggs again as a sign of Christ's resurrection. The shell of the egg could be seen as his tomb; breaking the egg represented Jesus rising from that tomb. The eggs were also dyed red, a reference to the blood of Christ. But this tradition was not new: the custom of dyeing eggs red in early spring had already been practised for centuries in China, Egypt and Persia.[1]

FIG. 1
Constantin Brancusi, *Le commencement du monde* (The Beginning of the World), 1924. Bronze, 16.5 × 28.5 × 15.5 cm. Kröller-Müller Museum, Otterlo.

Easter is not the only time for cracking eggs. The World Egg Organisation states on its website that global egg production rose from 61.7 billion kg in 2008 to 76.7 billion kg in 2018, a 24 per cent increase in ten years. Impressive figures, but how many eggs does that actually make? Let's do the maths: there are 15 to 25 eggs in a kilogram, depending on their size, so that's an almost incomprehensible 1,534,000,000,000. The website pluimveeweb.nl states that the average European ate 211 eggs in 2018. In Mexico, the average inhabitant consumes 360 eggs per year. In the Netherlands, we produce 10 billion eggs annually. And that's just chicken eggs, not counting geese, ducks and other birds.

The record egg layer in the seventeenth century was a duck, Sijctghen (cat. 16, p. 83), painted by Aelbert Cuyp (1620–1691). The lines written next to this black and white duck translate as follows:

> I was hatched at Werkendam.
> I was young and good when I came here
> into this bird stronghold. Without breeding
> I lived for 20 years.
> A hundred eggs I laid a year,
> which is why I have been painted.
> Broken bones, yet healed.
> Healthy am I, and piebald,
> and when I, Sijctghen, shall die,
> then write down how old, and the year 1647.
>
> In the year 1650, on 30 October,
> laments were heard
> on the death of Sijctghen;
> This is all true,
> being 23 years old in 1650.

'A hundred eggs I laid in a year, which is why I have been painted.' This very high number (for the time) was the occasion for the duck portrait. Sijctghen's great age when she died, 23, was also noteworthy, which is why this fact was added to the painting posthumously in 1650.

We humans eat not only eggs, but the chicken itself, which was domesticated 10,000 years ago. In the 1950s, chicken meat was still a rarity. Today, there are 99.9 million chickens in the Netherlands alone, most of which end up as food.[2] A Briton will eat on average 1,800 kg of chicken during their lifetime. An American will eat twice as much: 3,600 kg.[3] Of all the chickens we breed for meat, more than 70 per cent

FIG.2
Newly hatched chicks on a conveyor belt.

are slaughtered when they are 'fully grown'. That is not at the age of six, which is the average lifespan of a chicken, but after only six weeks. After that short period, the animals end up as chicken fillets in the supermarket, which you can buy for the price of a chocolate bar. Once a whole chicken is being roasted in the oven, it can finally enjoy a bit of space. The average Dutch hen lives with nine other hens on a single square metre,[4] while in intensive poultry farming, the number of hens can rise to 20 per square metre.[5]

The chicks raised on poultry farms are either used as broiler chickens (for meat) or become laying hens themselves (cat. 17, p. 84). This industry has no use for cockerels. Because they grow too slowly to be sold profitably as meat and because they don't lay eggs, the animals are ground or gassed shortly after birth. The hens are transported to laying farms or rearing farms. In the case of broiler chickens, the chicks grow at record speed to a weight of two kilos. In the Netherlands, broiler chickens may no longer be sold in supermarkets, but the wholesale trade still uses them extensively. A ban on breeding chickens that grow so fast they can't stand on their own legs will come into effect in 2040.

These chickens – our chickens – no longer eat crumbs of stale bread, as they did in the past, but feed made from soya beans. Of all the soya we produce worldwide, around 75 per cent is processed into animal feed. As the world's population continues to grow and as we consume more and more (chicken) meat and eggs, soya production increases too: by 1,500 per cent since the 1950s. The lion's share of soya comes from Brazil, with large-scale deforestation as a result. Every minute, eleven football fields of tropical rainforest disappear, the consequences of which we have long been aware of. The soya is then transported to Europe using highly polluting means of transport. To prevent all this, voices are being raised to feed our chickens only with leftovers from the food industry.

When it comes to eating poultry, the focus today is very much on chicken. The importance of this bird to us is reflected in the many proverbs and sayings about chickens and roosters to be found across numerous languages. Chicken is the most commonly eaten animal in the world, with between 137 and 205 million chickens consumed every day, depending on the source. Yet there are many other edible birds: partridge, pheasant, duck, goose, turkey, quail, pigeon and ostrich, to name but a few. In the seventeenth century, people in Europe also ate swans, peacocks, bitterns, redshanks, black-tailed godwits, lapwings, herons, storks, young gulls, snipes and curlews. Until the 1950s, eating starlings was also common.

David Teniers the Younger (1610–1690) painted this *Kitchen Interior* (cat. 13, pp. 78–79) with fish, roast meat, game and lots of poultry. These four foods represent the four elements (water, fire, earth, air). The showpiece is the swan pie on the table, decorated with symbols of love: a garland of red and white roses and a shield with a burning heart and two clasped hands. This work is Teniers' tribute to his wife, Anna, the seated woman who is casually peeling apples. Their six-year-old son David is holding the plate of apples. If we zoom in on the birds at the bottom left, we recognise, among others, a partridge, a pheasant and two kingfishers; there are also several birds, possibly thrushes, tied together on a stick. Some plucked poultry hangs in the top left corner, while birds are being roasted on a spit in the background.

Food historian Manon Henzen has created a contemporary swan pie (cat. 14, pp. 80–81). Not from ordinary swans, which are protected in the Netherlands, but from 'Schiphol swans', killed in collisions with aeroplanes. De Keuken van het Ongewenst Dier (The Kitchen of the Unwanted Animal), an organisation dedicated to eating animals that are killed through human activity, provided the swan to Henzen. She also advocates eating the geese that are gassed in huge numbers because of the nuisance they cause to air traffic around Schiphol Airport and the damage they cause to agricultural crops. To help guide us, she has made countless recipes from the past available; the one for swan pie can be found on her website: https://www.historicalcookingclasses.com/swan-pie/.

1 *Immaterieel Erfgoed* n.d.
2 *Nederland in cijfers* n.d.
3 *World Animal Protection* 2018.
4 *Beter leven. Dierenbescherming* n.d.
5 *Wakker dier* 2023.

Cat. 13

David Teniers II,
Kitchen Interior with Swan Pie, 1644.
Oil on copper, 55.5 × 77.5 cm.
Mauritshuis, The Hague, inv. no. 260.

Cat. 14

Manon Henzen,
Zwanenpastei (Swan Pie), 2025.
Taxidermy, metal, wheat flour,
sea salt, water, 95 × 135 cm.
Eet!verleden, Nijmegen.

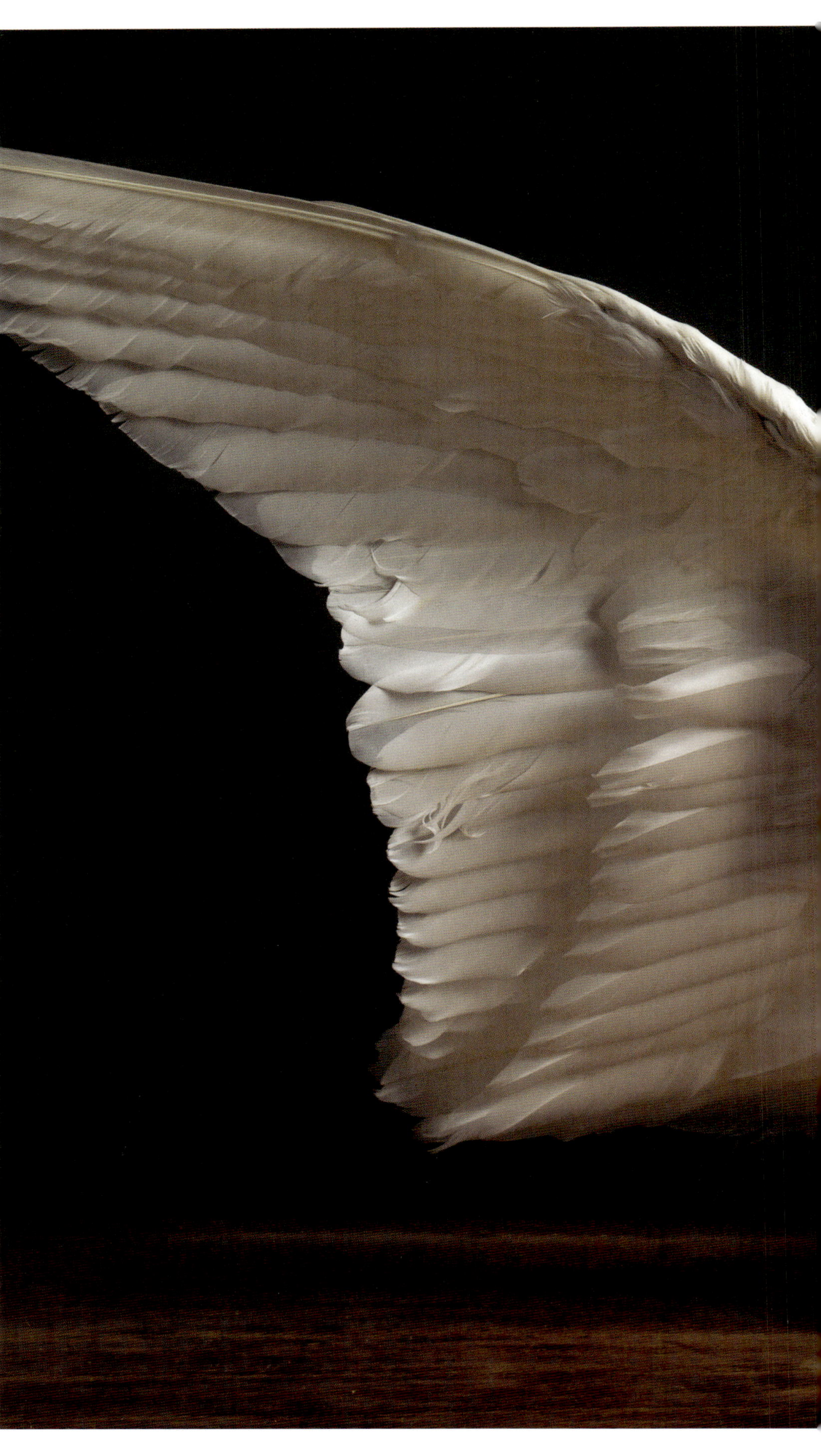

Cat. 15

Melchior d'Hondecoeter, *Seven Chicks*, c. 1665–1668. Oil on canvas, 32 × 38 cm. Rijksmuseum, Amsterdam, inv. no. SK-A-5023.

Cat. 16

Aelbert Cuyp, *Portrait of the Duck Sijctghen*, 1647–1650. Oil on panel, 35 × 41.5 cm. Dordrechts Museum, inv. no. DM/004/849.

Cat. 17

Still from *Our Daily Bread*, directed by Nikolaus Geyrhalter, 2005. HD CAM/35mm, 92 min.

Cat. 18

Tamara Kostianovsky, *Big Vulture*, 2016. Discarded and recycled textiles, 132 × 218 × 135 cm. Courtesy RX&SLAG, Paris/New York.

Plumage

Martine Gosselink

FIG. 1
Adolphe Millot, types of feathers, 1907–1910. Colour lithograph from *Le Larousse pour tous: Nouveau dictionnaire encyclopédique*, vol. 2, p. 465. Librairie Larousse, Paris.

Almost all adult birds have feathers (fig. 1). Consider the feather as an extension of the skin, in the same way that we have nails and hair and other animals have antlers or quills. A bird's body is covered with feathers for flying and display, but also for keeping warm. In particular, down feathers (*pluma* in Latin) are there to provide warmth and regulate moisture. Covert feathers streamline the bird's body and keep the down underneath dry. The sturdy remiges – the flight feathers in the wings – enable the bird to rise so that it they can fly. The rectrices – the flight feathers in the tail – are used for stability, steering and braking. Feathers are made of keratin, a tough, insoluble protein, which means they can be kept for a long time in a temperate climate, provided they are properly preserved.

Humans love feathers, not least because they serve several purposes. Since the sixth century, we have been using the outer flight feathers of geese and swans as writing materials (fig. 2). As soon as these birds lost their flight feathers during moulting – making them temporarily unable to fly – the feathers were collected to make quills. It was a truly disposable writing tool; after being trimmed too many times, one had no choice but to discard the goose feather. These organic writing instruments were commonplace until the nineteenth century, when they were replaced by modern pens (our word 'pen' comes from the Latin *penna*, meaning feather). In the following verse, Dutch poet Jacob Cats (1577–1660) expresses the view that the goose is little more than a supplier of pens:

FIG. 2
Gerard ter Borch, *The Letter Writer* (detail), c. 1655.
Oil on panel, 38.3 × 27.9 cm. Mauritshuis, The Hague.

> The goose, which almost has no brain,
> And lives by no art or wisdom,
> But does nothing else but
> To seek food in the green;
> It gives man the swift pen,
> The best gift that I know of.[1]

But we also use bird feathers in many other ways. Down and feathers have been utilised since time immemorial for their insulating properties. Feather-filled duvets made their appearance in Europe around 1300. The seventeenth-century English diplomat Paul Rycaut is said to have brought eiderdowns from the German territories to England, where the first use of the word duvet – the French word for down – was by the writer Samuel Johnson in 1759. Initially, only the nobility slept under down duvets. Since the twentieth century, however, they have become commonplace for many sleepers: in 2015, the BBC reported that 7.6 million duvets had been sold in the UK alone in the first half of that year. And let's not forget the immense numbers of feathers produced for pillows, thermal clothing and sleeping bags. Birds keep us warm!

Down quilts are articles of daily use nowadays. But in the past, the large-scale consumption of feathers served another purpose: as decoration or ornamentation to indicate one's social status. As early as the Palaeolithic period – also known as the Old Stone Age – feathers were used across the world in jewellery, musical instruments, weapons, clothing, masks, hats, headdresses and other head coverings. The inhabitants of the African continent were probably the first to do so.

Originating from Angola, this costume made of raffia and feathers (cat. 27, p. 102) is a rare nineteenth-century double-mask. The Wereldmuseum Leiden describes it as an Ndunga mask. It measures 175 cm high and comes from the Woyo or Vili, two related ethnic groups living on Angola's Loango coast. Like the Roman god Janus, the mask has two faces, painted in white, orange and black. Members of the Ndunga society who were allowed to wear these cloaks served the king and the most important spirits. The feathers on this object – which come from turacos (blue), sea eagles (black), hornbills (black and white) and guinea fowls (speckled white) as well as red-tailed parrots, great spotted cuckoos and roosters – offered protection to the spirits that had descended into the mask. Such protection may have been necessary since at the time when the mask was made, the territory of the Woyo and Vili was fraught due to border disputes, rivalries between neighbouring peoples, and colonial interference. The Ndunga mask was used to maintain order and for sentencing in relation to such matters. Ten similar masks are known worldwide, with six held in Dutch museums.

Around 1840, a Native American used the large feathers of a three-year-old eagle and the quills of a porcupine to make a headdress (cat. 21, p. 96). The bird was not chosen at random; an eagle's feathers brought wisdom to the wearer.

FIG. 3
Man's shirt, Plains Cree, US, c. 1840–1850. Antelope or deer skin, 115 × 165 cm. Wereldmuseum, Amsterdam/Leiden.

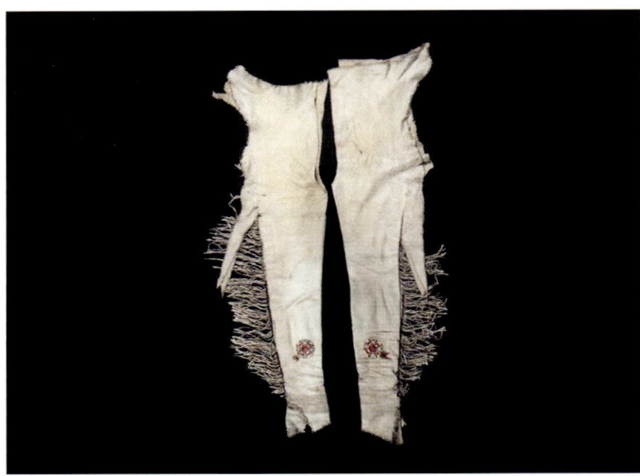

FIG. 4
Leggings, Plains Cree, US, c. 1840–1850. Antelope or deer skin, 132 × 34 cm. Wereldmuseum, Amsterdam/Leiden.

This type of feathered headband was quite common in eastern North America, where a branch of the Cree people lived on the Great Plains. Located east of the Rocky Mountains, these vast, treeless grasslands were home to nomadic peoples who travelled on horseback, lived in tipis and hunted bison. There are several early examples of such headdresses in museum collections in the Netherlands. However, this feathered headdress in the Wereldmuseum Leiden is possibly the only one from the Great Plains. Glued traces of red-dyed hair and white ermine fur can be observed on the tips of the feathers. The headdress was once purchased alongside a man's shirt and leggings made of animal skin (figs. 3 and 4). It is tempting to view these three items as forming a complete outfit worn by an inhabitant of the Great Plains in the mid-nineteenth century; in fact, their impeccable condition suggests that they were never worn. The Cree people associate the headdress with the identity of the person wearing it. Since they are made with bird feathers, the headdresses are considered living beings, and this sacred value must be respected. Present-day headdresses are made with turkey feathers, as eagle feathers are now protected.

Another headdress, made in the first half of the twentieth century (cat. 25, p. 100), has yellow and blue feathers. It was once worn by the Yñâ (Karajá), one of the four Indigenous groups to inhabit Bananal Island in central Brazil. It's the largest river island in the world – about the size of Sardinia. North of Bananal, where two river branches converge, is Cantão State Park, a unique nature reserve. This area of wetlands, where 700 bird species and almost 300 fish species have been observed, is one of the richest biological areas in the entire Amazon rainforest. The endangered giant otter, the black caiman and the arapaima gigas – one of the world's largest freshwater fish, which can grow up to three metres long – live there alongside the more common tapir, capybara, anaconda and jaguar. We don't know which of the 700 species of birds 'lent' their feathers for this headdress.

It was probably around the mid-nineteenth century that an Ecuadorian headdress maker from the Gâ'tɨya pâín (also known as the Siona community) attached a beige headband with little feathers to a double braided band, decorated with reddish-green, reddish-yellow and yellow feathers (cat. 26, p. 101). A wonderfully long tail of green feathers was then attached to this headdress. The Siona live between the Putumayo River and its tributaries in the Amazon region of Colombia and Ecuador, where their way of life has been turned upside down since the discovery of oil and as a result of the effects of globalisation. Like other Indigenous peoples of the Americas, they use feathers for healing purposes. The decline of bird populations in the Amazon is putting these traditions at risk.

The fact that feathers have not only spiritual worth but can also be of great financial value was evident on 21 May 2024 when a tail feather from an extinct bird, at least a

FIG. 5
A Maori tribal chief with a huia feather in his hair.

hundred years old, was auctioned in New Zealand for more than 26,000 euros, a record amount. The blackish-brown feather with a distinctive white tip came from a huia, a New Zealand songbird last seen in 1907. Only Maori chiefs and their immediate family members would allowed to wear huia feathers, which were revered and carefully preserved in special boxes (fig. 5). Once European collectors became keen to get their hands on the huia's feathers – apparently after the Duke of York wore one in his hat during a visit to New Zealand in 1901 – the bird rapidly became extinct.[2]

Feathers have been important to many populations, from Africa to the Americas, both ceremonially and aesthetically. Millions of pieces of historic clothing and other artefacts integrating feathers are now stored in the depots of ethnographic museums, mainly in Europe and North America.[3]

Bird feathers were an integral part of everyday and sacred attire in Europe too. We don't know exactly when Europeans began to adorn themselves with feathers, but it was probably also in the Palaeolithic period. Remains of sea eagles and ospreys have been found in various prehistoric and Roman settlements in the Netherlands, the birds having probably been killed for their plumage. The Greeks and Romans decorated their helmets with metal wings or feathered crests, primarily for identification and to intimidate their enemies. The personification of Roma was portrayed with wings on her helmet, like Hermes, the messenger of the gods in Greek mythology (the Roman equivalent being Mercury), whose sandals were fitted with wings.

In sixteenth-century Europe, small feathers were fashionable, but one century later, the bigger and fuller the better. Large plumes were also popular during the Baroque period. Visual proof of this is to be found in Rembrandt's *Tronie of a Man with a Feathered Beret* (cat. 20, p. 95). The artist depicts a soldier dressed in an old-fashioned style. This is not a portrait of a specific person, but a *tronie*, or character sketch. No less extravagant are the feathers on the lovely head of Caspar Netscher's bubble-blowing boy (fig. 6). Although the painting is tiny, the ruffles, curls, ribbons, bow tie, collar and, of course, bright blue ostrich feather are rendered with tremendous precision. The youthful lad and his soap bubble are a warning to us, a reminder of how short life can be, how it can burst like a soap bubble. In the Netherlands, we are still reminded today of the exuberant fashion for feathers in the seventeenth century: indeed, the feather on the beret of 'Piet', the helper who accompanies St Nicholas, is, after all, a nineteenth-century invention, copied from the clothing worn by pages in the seventeenth century.

In the eighteenth century, the love of feathers could take on decadent forms. Absurdly tall wigs were adorned with feathers and often raised higher still. An etching from around 1775 makes fun of a French lady walking through London. She wears a gigantic wig on her head that is home to pigeons that an English hunter is taking aim at (fig. 7).

FIG. 6
Caspar Netscher, *A Boy Blowing Bubbles*, 1670.
Oil on panel, 11.2 × 8.4 cm. Mauritshuis, The Hague, on loan from Rob Vellekoop, since 2011.

FIG. 7
Anonymous, *Mlle des Faveurs à Londres* (Miss des Faveurs in London), c. 1775. Etching, 342 × 248 mm. Musée du Louvre, Paris.

FIG. 8
John Collet, *The Preposterous Head Dress, or the Feathered Lady*, 1776. Hand-coloured engraving, 354 × 251 mm. The British Museum, London.

The accompanying poem can be translated as:

> My hairstyle does indeed resemble a dovecote,
> Since all those pigeons come there to rest,
> But what are you doing, Englishman, shooting at them?
> Must you act recklessly on account of our foolishness?

The print *The Preposterous Head Dress, or the Feathered Lady* dates from the same period (fig. 8). It shows a wig decked like a Christmas tree with ostrich feathers. In another satirical print, ostriches, angry at having been plucked bare, take revenge on the young ladies displaying their feathers (fig. 9). Mocking outlandish fashion trends featuring feathers was clearly already in vogue at the end of the eighteenth century, though not because of any suffering caused to the birds.

That changed in the Netherlands in 1892, when the aristocratic sisters Cécile and Elsa de Jong van Beek en Donk founded the Bond ter Bestrijding eener Gruwelmode (Society for the Abolition of Cruel Fashion). Their aim was to denounce the use of bird feathers in hats and other items of clothing. Queen Emma supported the principles of the society, which quickly attracted hundreds of members. A few years later, in 1899, the Netherlands became the first country in Europe to establish a national bird conservation organisation, the Vereeniging tot Bescherming van Vogels (Society for the Protection of Birds). Thirteen years later, all wild birds

FIG. 9
John Collet, *The Feather'd Fair in a Fright*, c. 1777. Mezzotint, 356 × 253 mm. The British Museum, London.

in the Netherlands were protected by law. How did this happen? How did this movement suddenly gain in popularity and become successful, so soon after it was established? The explanation lies in the cruel fashion mentioned above. Vast numbers of birds were being killed in order to decorate hats with their feathers; some ladies even displayed dead birds on their headwear (fig. 10): terns, kingfishers, pheasants, egrets and goldfinches. When the Society for the Protection of Birds was founded, hats like this pink and green feather version were popular, combining what was probably the head of a bird of paradise with feathers from hummingbirds and other tropical birds (cat. 24, pp. 98–99). The mounting of hummingbird wings and bird-of-paradise tails became a craze, a trend that led to the death of hundreds of thousands of birds every year. A folding fan with bright pink ostrich feathers (cat. 23, p. 97) and another with monal feathers (cat. 22, pp. 96–97) – so striking on account of their iridescent sheen – date from the early twentieth century. Opposition to this practice was just as strong as the urge to continue wearing feather hats, fans and boas; witness the satirical image of a woman wearing a yellow dress and an enormous feathered hat who smiles as she aims her rifle at several white birds (fig. 11). Two dogs with human faces bring more dead birds to the pile at the woman's feet. At the time, some believed the woman resembled Coco Chanel – the caption on the cartoon reads 'French milliner'.

Although the helmet of comic book hero Asterix, the plucky little warrior from Gaul, is decorated with feathers, Gaulish helmets with wings have rarely been found during archaeological digs. Asterix's wings are a romantic fantasy dating from the nineteenth century, just like horns on Viking helmets. The Gauls may not have worn feathers on their helmets, but history is full of examples of plumage displayed by the military. They not only gave warriors and soldiers strength, but also indicated their rank, depending on the feathers' shape, size and colour. Feathers still appear on military uniforms, usually attached to helmets as plumes.

FIG. 10
Mannequin wearing a hat with a tern.

FIG. 11
Gordon Ross, *The Woman Behind the Gun*, 1911.
Photomechanical print, offset, colour.
Library of Congress, Washington DC.

They were also used to embellish diplomats' attire, as in the case of the hat with upright white ostrich feathers that was part of an ambassador's uniform in the mid-twentieth century (cat. 19, p. 94).

Indeed, it is striking how often ostrich feathers were used throughout the centuries. Ostriches from across Africa and the Middle East were plucked bare to supply them. Nowadays, ostriches are only found in South Africa and East Africa. The South African city of Oudtshoorn grew rich in the nineteenth century from the mass export of ostrich feathers; the ostrich farms are still there today, but now the birds are mainly bred for leather and meat. The farmers, it seems, are still feathering their nests.

1 Mantingh 2022, pp. 71–72.
2 *VRT NWS* 2024.
3 We recognise that Indigenous groups from other continents have been alienated from their own heritage due to, among other things, the collecting and Christianisation practices of Europeans. It is particularly regrettable that the communities to whom these objects once belonged have little or no access to them today. These topics are very important, but outside the scope of this book.

Cat. 19

Jones, Chalk & Dawson Ltd., Headdress of Ambassador Allard Merens, c. 1945–1976. Textile, metal, feathers, 18 × 57 cm. Rijksmuseum, Amsterdam, inv. no. NG-1976-13-A-6.

Cat. 20

Rembrandt, *Tronie of a Man with a Feathered Beret*, c. 1635–1640. Oil on panel, 62.5 × 47 cm. Mauritshuis, The Hague, inv. no. 149.

Cat. 21

Headdress, Plains Cree, US, c. 1840. Skin, porcupine quills, eagle feathers, ermine, hair, pigment, 42 × 18 cm. Wereldmuseum, Amsterdam/Leiden, inv. no. RMV 524-1.

Cat. 22

Fan with iridescent pheasant feathers on a frame of imitation tortoiseshell with cord and silk tassel, c. 1900–1910.
Feathers, plastic, silk, steel, 16 × 28 cm (open).
Rijksmuseum, Amsterdam, inv. no. BK-1969-53.

Cat. 23

Folding fan with bright pink ostrich feathers on a plain plastic frame with tortoiseshell pattern, c.1900–1925.
Ostrich feathers, plastic, 69 × 88 cm (open).
Rijksmuseum, Amsterdam, inv. no. BK-1969-52-A.

Cat. 24

Hat feather composed of the mounted head of a bird of paradise (?) and feathers from hummingbird and other tropical birds, c. 1910–1915. Feathers, 25 × 12 × 33 cm. Rijksmuseum, Amsterdam, inv. no. BK-1967-56.

Cat. 25

Headdress of yellow and blue feathers, Karajá, Brazil, before 1956. Feathers, plant fibre, 40 × 40 × 32 cm. Wereldmuseum, Amsterdam/Leiden, inv. no. TM-2479-1.

Cat. 26

Feather headdress, presumably worn by a Siona (Cushman) man, Ecuador, 1983. Bark, bone, cotton fibre, feather, braids, wool, 87 × 35 × 30 cm. Wereldmuseum, Amsterdam/Leiden, inv. no. TM-4825-1.

Cat. 27

Feather costume with double mask, Cabinda, Angola, late 19th century. Wood, bird feathers, pigment, raffia, 175 × 110 × 50 cm. Wereldmuseum Rotterdam, inv. no. WM-28548.

Cat. 28

Iris van Herpen, 'Idolomantis', *Roots of Rebirth Collection*, look 17, 2021. Duchess fabric, organza, mylar foil, cotton. Atelier Iris van Herpen, Amsterdam.

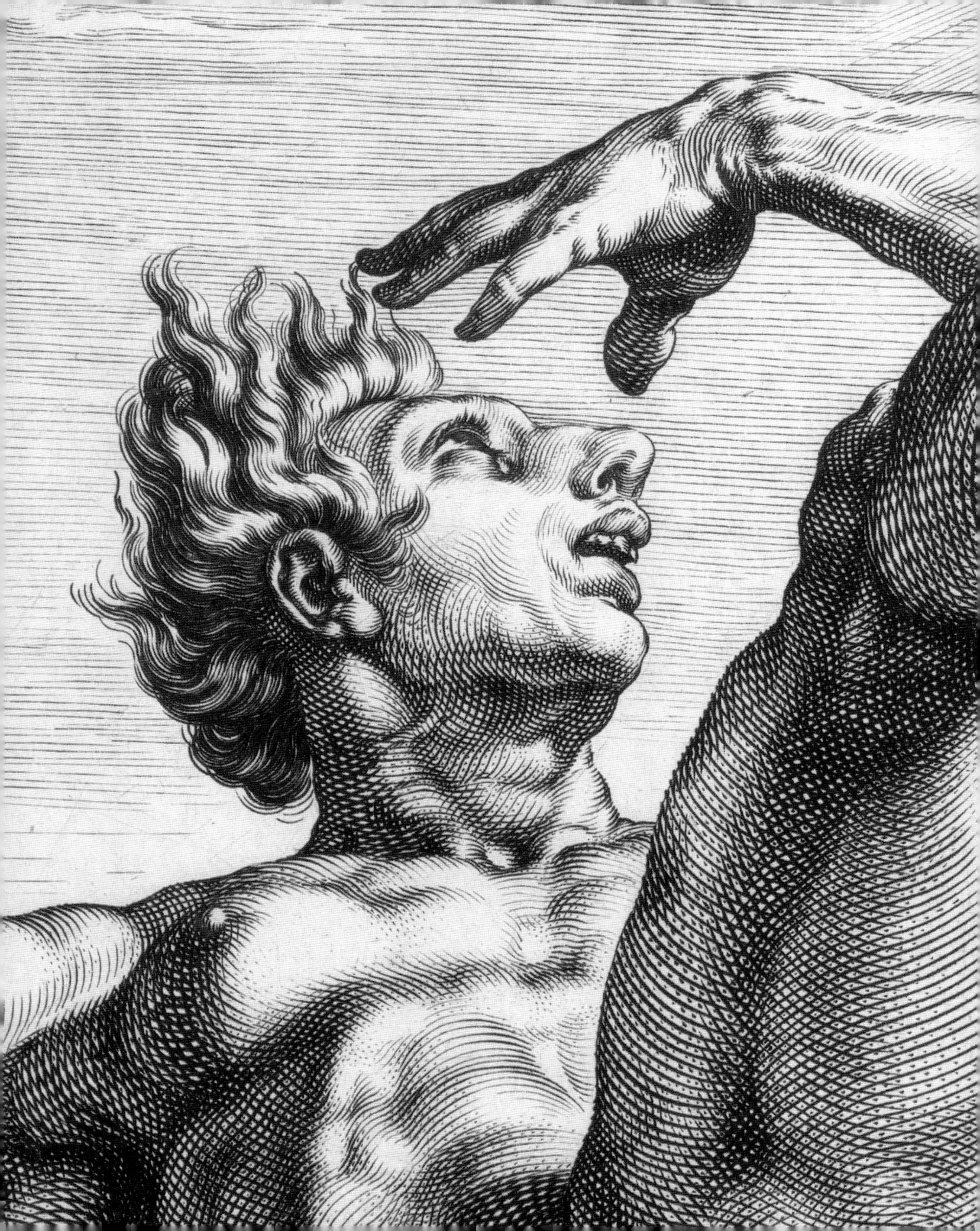

Envying Avians

Martine Gosselink

FIG. 1
Albrecht Dürer, *Wing of a Blue Roller*, c. 1500. Watercolour and gouache on parchment, 196 × 200 mm. Albertina, Vienna.

We humans can do quite a lot: walk, run, crawl, swim, jump, climb and clamber. But flying? Nothing doing. It is precisely because we know we will never be able to fly that we desire it even more and envy those creatures that can. This is why we see it as something supernatural, magical, spiritual. No wonder wing tattoos on shoulder blades are so popular. The idea of being able to lift oneself off the ground under one's own power – give or take a running start or leap – and then fly, float or flutter through the air has inspired many a writer, poet, artist and scientist. Our tales and stories feature numerous flying characters, from Icarus, Peter Pan and Harry Potter to Superman, Mary Poppins and Aladdin. Some fly under their own power, others rely on a broomstick, umbrella or carpet.

In his timeless *Metamorphoses*, the Roman poet Ovid breathed new life into the already ancient myth of Daedalus and his son Icarus. A skilled architect and craftsman, Daedalus built a complex labyrinth for King Minos of Crete. Fearing that Daedalus would reveal secret knowledge about the labyrinth, Minos imprisoned him along with his son. The only way to escape was by air. The ingenious Daedalus studied the birds in the sky, collected their feathers and created wings so that they could fly away from the island. You can read what happens next on p. 190. The story of Daedalus and Icarus has inspired countless artists over hundreds of years to create flying or falling Icaruses. Henri Matisse (1869–1954) has the boy dropping through a blue night filled with twinkling stars (cat. 29, pp. 108–109), while Hendrick Goltzius (1558–1617) depicts him tumbling to the ground – as if humankind as a whole had fallen (cat. 33, p. 111).

Like Daedalus, Albrecht Dürer (1471–1528) studied birds and collected feathers. In 1506, he was asked by his friend Willibald Pirckheimer to buy feathers when he reached Venice, where birds and feathers from all corners of the world were traditionally offered for sale at the market.[1] It goes without saying that feathers and wings appealed to artists who portrayed angels in their paintings. There is no better expression of humankind's fascination with feathers than Dürer's watercolour *Wing of a Blue Roller* (fig. 1). The European roller is one of around twelve species (family *Coraciidae)* found in Africa, Asia and Europe. Although Dürer would have intended this drawing as a study, it is a work of art in its own right. The colours are astonishing: seven shades can be distinguished in the green alone. From sturdy flight feathers to soft down: each feather is built up in detail from barbs that visibly interlock. The shorter coverts overlap the down in a tight pattern, while the brown feathers are grouped in tufts next to the (missing) breast of the roller – a bird that Dürer also drew in its entirety, for that matter (fig. 3, p. 170).

FIG. 2
Albrecht Dürer, *Nemesis (Das große Gluck)* (Nemesis [The Great Happiness]), c. 1501. Coloured copper engraving, 339 × 231 mm. Staatliche Museen zu Berlin, Berlin.

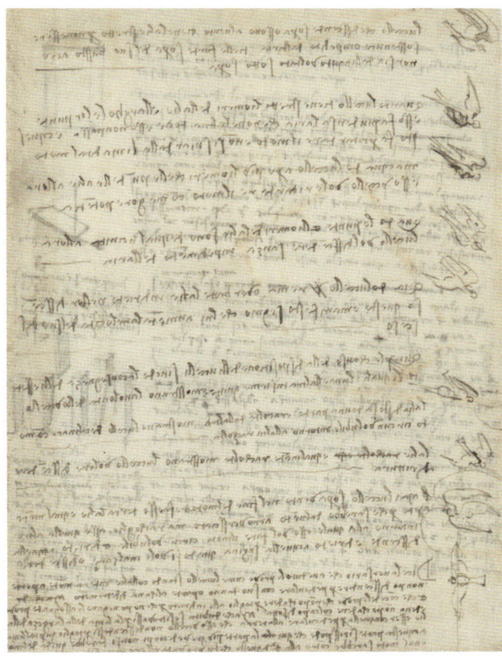

FIG. 3
Leonardo da Vinci, *Codex Atlanticus*, fol. 185r, c. 1478–1518. Pen and ink on paper, 645 × 435 mm. Biblioteca Ambrosiana, Milan.

Feather studies such as this are important if you want to learn how to represent angel wings convincingly. Dürer's *Nemesis* is an exceptional achievement in this regard (fig. 2), both in the colour gradations and in the lengths of the different types of feathers. Dürer used black paint to lend depth and weight to Nemesis's splendid plumage, while green pigments provide its iridescent sheen. Here, Dürer combines Nemesis, the goddess of vengeance and retribution (with lidded urn and bridle), with the winged Fortuna, standing on her globe. The landscape beneath the figure is breathtaking: a grand panorama in, yes, a bird's-eye view. It is tempting to assume that Dürer not only drew birds and wings, but also tried to put himself in the creatures' place by drawing landscapes from above, the way they see them from the air. The depiction of landscapes from a bird's-eye view was starting to enter European cartography at that time. Dürer may have seen this valley from a mountain top during a trip to Italy. Did he perhaps envy the birds their vast field of vision?

Like Daedalus, the artist-inventor Leonardo da Vinci (1452–1519) wanted to take flight. Convinced that humans could fly, he studied the flight movements of birds, their feathers, their wings and how they were attached to the bird's body (cats. 31 and 32, p. 110). In his *Codex Atlanticus*, a collection of his drawings and writing, which runs to hundreds of pages, he devoted several notes to birds (fig. 3). As a child, Da Vinci (who may have been a vegetarian) admired birds; he would buy caged birds at the market and then set them free.[2] His earliest flight-related designs consisted of sets of wings that one could put on. In vain. Da Vinci eventually understood that the seemingly effortless defiance of gravity required an amount of energy that humans simply do not possess. For many birds, it is, incidentally, quite a strenuous exercise: their wings must be beaten up and down with great speed and rhythm. Imagine you are a well-fed goose: how powerful would your muscles have to be to get your body moving? Once in the air, large birds such as condors and albatrosses barely move their wings; they rely almost exclusively on the power of the wind to soar. But to get off the ground, and this is what it comes down to, they need great muscle power. No wonder that in some birds the chest muscles can make up to 25 per cent of their total body weight.

When Da Vinci concluded that human muscle power in the chest and arms was insufficient to lift one off the ground, he designed his flying machines in such a way that a person could use their legs. At the same time, he still based his designs on avian aerodynamics. This modified methodology was also unsuccessful, but it was a source of inspiration for the mechanical engineers who invented the first flying machines in the twentieth century. In 1903, the Wright brothers, who also studied the balancing skills of birds in the wind, succeeded in keeping a machine in the air. Da Vinci had predicted it!

Like Daedalus and Da Vinci, the modern aircraft industry also looks to birds. Their hollow feathers and bones, lung capacity, streamlined movements, navigational abilities, energy consumption, manoeuvrability and use of air currents are all elements that are incorporated into the design of contemporary aircraft. The raised tips at the ends of the aircraft's wings (winglets), for example, are modelled on the way birds bend their wings while flying. The Dutch airline KLM showcased the graceful swan and its immense power in numerous advertisements from 1992 to 1998 (cat. 30, p. 109). In this way, the swan – an emblem of reliability, care and elegance – became for years the quintessential symbol of national pride. By imitating bird aerodynamics, we have come a long way and can now fly around the world – but still not under our own power, something birds have been able to do for 150 million years. Only dreams in which we can fly – which indicate the processing of long-standing problems or major worries – are we able to glide above forests, fields and rivers using only our own bodies as instruments.

Birds also symbolise freedom and lightness – 'free as a bird', as the phrase goes – and for good reason. The fact that they can travel anywhere they want is indeed an enviable quality; borders, walls and territorial airspace do not exist for them. The association with lightness has to do with their very light feathers and wings, and the very weightlessness of some birds. If you have ever held a great tit (average weight 18g) or wren (7–12g) in your hand, you will have barely noticed its weight.

In the Dutch language, our admiration, tinged with envy, for birds and their freedom does have its limits. Indeed, while we may use the phrase *als een vogel zo vrij* ('free as a bird'), we also have the word *vogelvrij*, whose literal translation, 'bird-free', is at some remove from its actual meaning: 'outlaw'. People declared *vogelvrij*, such as William of Orange and Robin Hood, were deprived of the protection of the law; as a result, anyone could kill them without fear of prosecution. The status of a person declared *vogelvrij* was comparable to that of certain birds. Crows, for example, which damaged crops, could in the past be shot with impunity – a measure that did not apply to other birds. How ironic that a person declared *vogelvrij*, if killed, ultimately served as carrion for the birds in the open air on the gallows field.

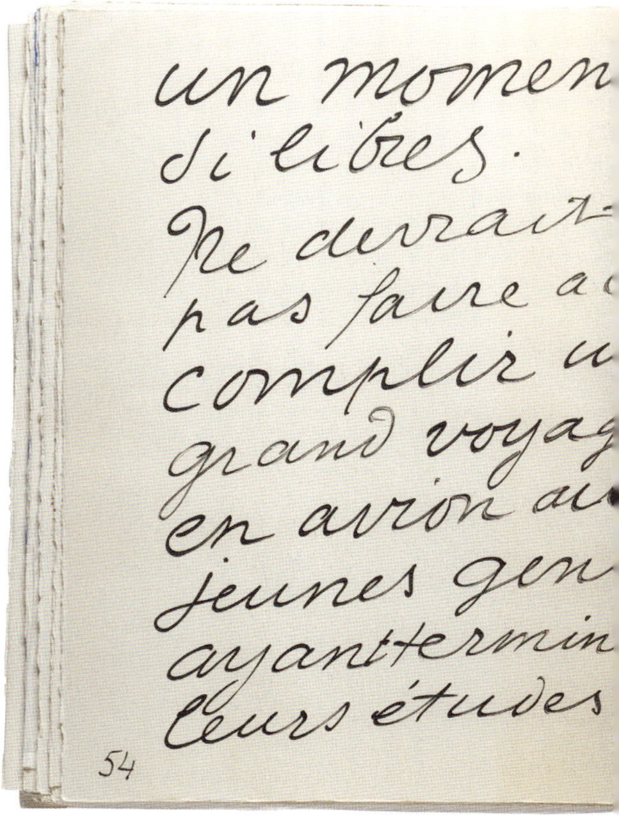

1 Schleif 2010, p. 202.
2 Kane 2002.

Cat. 29

Henri Matisse, *Icarus*, 1947. Pochoir print from *Jazz*, 421 × 326 mm. Museum Voorlinden, Wassenaar, inv. no. M00305.

Cat. 30

Swan, KLM commercial, 1995. Video, 40 sec. KLM Heritage Centre, Amstelveen.

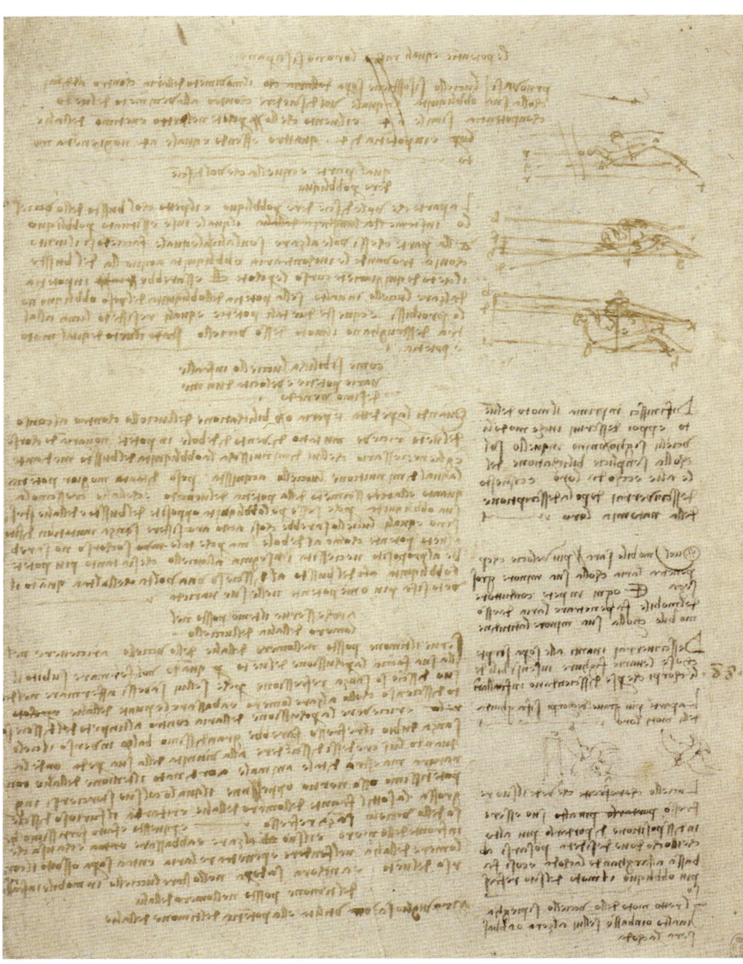

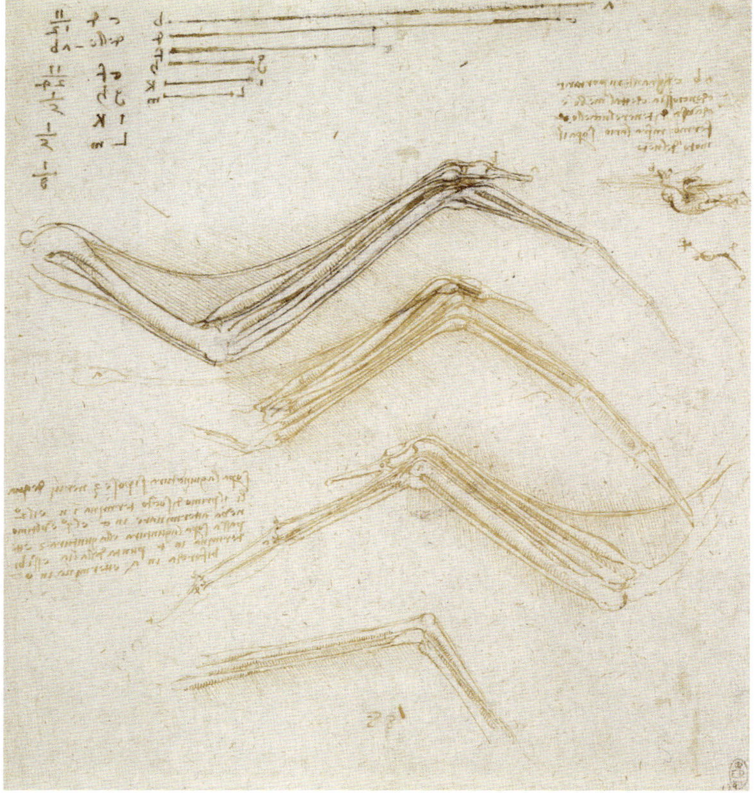

Cat. 31

Leonardo da Vinci, *Notes on Flying Birds*, c. 1511–1513. Pen and ink on paper, 272 × 208 mm. The Royal Collection/ HM King Charles III, inv. no. RCIN 912657.

Cat. 32

Leonardo da Vinci, *The Anatomy of a Bird's Wing*, c. 1512. Black chalk, pen and ink on paper, 222 × 204 mm. The Royal Collection/ HM King Charles III,, inv. no. RCIN 912656.

Cat. 33

Hendrick Goltzius after a design by Cornelis Cornelisz. van Haarlem, *Icarus*, 1588.
Engraving from the series *The Four Fliers*, 327 mm (diam.).
Rijksmuseum, Amsterdam, inv. no. RP-P-OB-10.363.

The Genius of Birds

Martine Gosselink

Birds are superior creatures. Their genius is beyond our comprehension, not only because it cannot be measured, but because we are still far from having fully understood how their brains work. And we as humans want to understand birds, in order to learn from them and make the most of this acquired knowledge in our own scientific models. Take the navigational abilities of birds, for example. Back in antiquity, the Greeks and Romans used pigeons to deliver messages by attaching rolled-up pieces of paper to their legs. The Abbasid caliphs (750–1258), who ruled from Spain to Central Asia, communicated via carrier pigeon and had a network of dovecotes across their empire. In the tenth century, the fifth Fatimid caliph, Al-Aziz, who loved cherries from Baalbek in Lebanon, reportedly had 600 pigeons fly from Cairo to Baalbek and back again, each carrying a single cherry. In many wars throughout history, carrier pigeons were relied on to carry messages across enemy zones to army camps. Young pigeons are trained by having them fly back to their own pigeon coop from ever greater distances; they seem to have a built-in compass, but exactly how it works is something that science has not yet discovered.

Migratory birds trust this compass to travel annually from point A to point B. They set off from the place where they hatched their eggs for a region where sufficient food can be found in winter. In the extreme case of the Arctic tern, this journey will take them from the Arctic to the Antarctic and then back again for the next breeding season, a round-trip distance that amounts to some 70,000 kilometres (!) per year. How exactly does bird navigation work? This varies according to species and can be a combination of several systems. These include a built-in biological clock, being able to perceive changes in the weather, the presence of food, the position of the stars and the Sun, the influence of the Earth's magnetic field (compass function) and features of the landscape for orientation purposes (waterways, mountains, deserts, forests). But are we any wiser for all that?

In the 1950s, Dutch biologist Ab Perdeck conducted some fascinating research into the migration of starlings. Together with his colleagues, he caught 11,000 starlings on their way west from the Netherlands. They ringed the birds and took them to Schiphol Airport, from where they were transported by plane in a south-easterly direction to Switzerland, where they were released. Perdeck wanted to know how the starlings would complete their journey. Would they correct the change in direction themselves and manage to reach their original destination? If so, it would mean they had detailed knowledge to guide them. Or would they continue flying as if the change of course to Switzerland had never occurred? In that case, this would (only) demonstrate the existence of an internal compass.

It turned out that the young birds with no experience did indeed rely on their internal compass. They followed an innate, inbuilt travel programme (nature) and ended up at a completely different location from where the colony normally wintered. In contrast, the adult starlings reached their usual wintering grounds because they managed to adjust their route. The older birds had apparently learned from previous experience and were able to adapt their travel plans (nurture).[1]

It is a spectacle that can be admired year after year: the marvellous aerial display of countless starlings, sometimes numbering in their thousands, performing an aerial ballet as if they were a single organism. These synchronised flocks of starlings are called murmurations (cat. 34, pp. 116–117), after the French verb *murmurer* (to murmur, whisper, babble). That murmuring is the sound made by a dancing-flying colony of starlings flapping their wings. Have you ever seen one? Then you must have asked yourself: who's leading the dance, who's the choreographer? How is it possible that thousands of birds can move together without colliding into one another? If you have never witnessed a murmuration, you should visit the marshy areas of the Netherlands between November and February, when there are as many starlings wintering in the country as there are human inhabitants. At dusk, small groups of birds seek each other out. The flock swells and swells, until darkness falls and the show comes to a sudden halt: then they dive towards their place of rest in one swoop to roost for the night.

No single bird is in charge of the murmuration. The starlings start and move together. It is always a different bird that sets a new direction, the others following. Each starling pays close attention to the movements of seven of its neighbours. Apparently, that is enough to avoid them touching each other while staying in step. What also helps is that they all fly at exactly the same speed, 36 kilometres per hour. No bird has to slow down or speed up unnecessarily, which also prevents them from crashing into each other.

The mesmerising air ballets that starlings treat us to also have a function. By flying in such a large group, the birds form a vast cloud that attracts the attention of others, who then join in. As a large group, they are less likely to be attacked by birds of prey than if they were alone – so, as night falls, it is much safer for them to be together. Also, the enemy (the bird of prey) is more easily spotted by thousands of starling eyes. The following morning, the birds break up into smaller groups to search for food. This is a truly unique form of collaboration.

The diversity of bird nests is equally phenomenal – and fascinating. An endless variety of nests can be found in all kinds of places: in trees, roof gutters and chimneys as well as on water and among reeds. These nests can be made from all sorts of materials, ranging from grass, feathers, moss and twigs to polystyrene, rope and plastic waste. Each bird species has its own type of nest. Blackbirds and finches build their bowl-shaped nests in tree forks or hedges; sparrows prefer to make their homes beneath roof tiles; woodpeckers and tits are fond of hollow tree trunks; herons and storks like to nest on raised platforms; the great spotted woodpecker carves its nest in the hardest tree; swallows make cup-shaped nests out of clay.

And then there are the weavers, birds named after the way they make their spherical nests, namely, by weaving. Male weavers use their beaks to 'sew' blades of grass into an ingenious hanging structure (fig. 1). This takes them about two days. The female weavers add the finishing touches, lining the interior of the nest with down and fluff. Sometimes you will find several weaver nests in one tree. Namibia is home to the largest weaver nests in the world, built collectively and often used for several years in a row. The birds enter these giant nests – which can accommodate an entire weaver colony – from below or the side.

Then there are the nests made by humans – we have been building dovecotes, birdhouses and nest boxes for centuries. But are birds keen on such man-made dwellings? According to nature organisations, they are, because more and more birds are having trouble finding suitable nesting sites. This is partly the result of human activity: we insulate our houses, use unsuitable roof designs, replace hedges with wooden fences. The common house sparrow (the name says it all) is much less common than it used to be; according to Vogelbescherming Nederland (Society for the Protection of Birds, Netherlands), the country's house sparrows have declined by more than 50% since 1975.

The nest that wins the top prize for the most wonderful bird dwelling ever is, surely, a magpie nest kept in the Naturalis Biodiversity Center's collection in Leiden (cat. 36, p. 120). Why? Because the pair of magpies in question built it out of anti-bird spikes, which are intended to deter birds. Conservator and biologist Auke-Florian Hiemstra retrieved the nest from a tree in the grounds of the University Hospital Antwerp in the autumn of 2021. It had been built in the spring of that year, but was then abandoned by the magpie family. Hiemstra was particularly impressed by the strength and size of the nest, which had a kind of roof to provide extra protection for the magpies' eggs and chicks.

FIG. 1
Male Baya Weaver (*Ploceus philippinus*) attracts a female bird in the breeding colony.

1 Birkhead 2008, pp. 133–176.

Cat. 34

Previous pages: Jan van IJken,
The Art of Flying, 2015. HD video, black & white,
6 min 52 sec. Jan van IJken, Beesd.

Cat. 35

Anonymous, Glass pane with a chained goldfinch
in front of a birdhouse, Netherlandish, c. 1650–1675.
Grisaille paint on glass, 11.6 × 8.4 cm.
Rijksmuseum, Amsterdam, inv. no. BK-LXXXI-L.

LXXXI l.

Cat. 36

Magpies, Composite nest, 2021. Anti-bird spikes, 85 × 70 × 80 cm. Naturalis Biodiversity Center, Leiden, inv. no. RMNH.AVES.259588.

Cat. 37

Constantin Brancusi, *L'Oiseau dans l'espace* (Bird in Space), 1932–1940. Brass, 151 cm high. Peggy Guggenheim Collection, Venice, inv. no. 76.2553.51.

Heavenly Messengers

Martine Gosselink

Whether institutionalised or popular, centred on a god or on nature, every religion, every belief system, has assigned meaning to birds. Simply because birds, given their ability to fly, move between heaven and earth and can therefore be seen as divine messengers or as the embodiment of the spiritual. Alongside magical birds, mythologies feature countless other winged creatures: the Sphinx, the wind demon Pazuzu from Mesopotamia, Canaanite demons, the monumental bull Lamassu that guarded the city gates in Assyria, flying dragons, the horse Pegasus, the three Greek harpies, the Greek goddess Nike, the Lion of Venice, and the more contemporary Falkur, the 'luck dragon' from the 1979 novel *The Neverending Story.* These fabled creatures accompany protagonists on their adventures, grant extraordinary powers and provide insight. In the Bible, Psalm 91:4–6 gives God metaphorical wings that offer shelter: 'He shall cover thee with his feathers, and under his wings shalt thou trust: his truth shall be thy shield and buckler. Thou shalt not be afraid for the terror by night; nor for the arrow that flieth by day; Nor for the pestilence that walketh in darkness; nor for the destruction that wasteth at noonday.'

In the Bible, it is the cherubim and seraphim that are winged, not the angels. When the latter want to visit God in heaven, they simply climb a ladder. It was not until the fourth century that angels were given wings in Christian iconography.[1] By the time that Peter Paul Rubens (1577–1640) depicted Mary being accompanied on her ascent to heaven by some strapping putti and angels (cat. 38, p. 131), their winged nature had been a given for centuries. Mary rises from a stone sarcophagus towards heaven as if caught in a light-grey whirlwind, with Rubens' powerful brushstrokes adding an extra twist to the swirling column of air.

One of the world's oldest surviving religions is Zoroastrianism, whose supreme deity, Ahura Mazda, is a winged male figure. Zoroastrianism is considered to be the first religion to have developed a dualistic antagonism between good and evil. When humans struggle with themselves, they must always choose what is right, which rests on three simple pillars: good thoughts, good words and good deeds. The religion adopted existing traditions from the wider region, such as ritual singing and the cult of fire. By gradually designating the god Ahura Mazda as the sole god, Zoroastrianism became a monotheistic faith. Ahura Mazda is recognisable by his outstretched wings (fig. 1). In Iran, it is still possible to visit flat-roofed towers on which the corpses of Zoroastrians were left for the vultures. Indeed, the Zoroastrians believed that the human body, once death had occurred, could immediately be taken over by evil spirits. To prevent this from happening, the remains were exposed to natural elements – that is, to vultures. Since the 1970s, Zoroastrians, now a small minority, have been prohibited from performing this ritual in Iran.

Over the past few decades, large numbers of vultures on the Indian subcontinent have died, mainly due to unintentional poisoning by the anti-inflammatory drug diclofenac,

FIG. 1
Stone-carved Ahura Mazda in Persepolis, Iran, c. 6000–4000 BCE.

FIG. 2
Gioacchino Assereto, *The Torture of Prometheus*, 1620–1648. Oil on canvas, 83 × 69.5 cm. Musée de la Chartreuse, Douai.

which is widely administered to livestock in India and Pakistan. As a result, in this area too, the centuries-old ritual of offering bodies to the birds – known as sky burial, and based on the principle of not polluting the earth – comes to a tragic end.[2]

This mummified falcon (cat. 43, p. 136) from the Ptolemaic period (332–30 BCE) of ancient Egypt served as a mediator between people on earth and the world of the gods. Millions of mummified animals have been excavated in Egypt, many with messages that the animal was intended to convey to the realm of the gods. Falcons (and other animals) were specially bred for this purpose on temple grounds; they were sold to visitors and then sacrificed by a priest. This falcon was found in an animal cemetery in Saqqara, in northern Egypt.

The ancient Egyptians believed that every human being has an immortal soul, the *ba*. When a person dies, the *ba* – usually represented in the form of a bird with a human head – is able to leave the tomb and make its way to the world of the living, but only during the day; at night, the soul is reunited with the body. Wooden statuettes, such as this one (cat. 46, p. 139) dating from the Late period (664–332 BCE), often accompanied burials, usually being placed on the lid of the coffin. The sun disc on the figurine's head may refer to the sky, the avian realm. Golden pendants in the shape of birds with outstretched wings similar to Ahura Mazda served the same function (cat. 45, p. 138). Such amulets were interpreters of the soul, moving freely between the living and the body in the tomb.

In ancient Greece, the story of how the king of the Olympian gods, Zeus, came into conflict with Prometheus, son of an earlier Titan god, proves that birds are not always positive messengers in mythology. Prometheus created humans out of clay, and gave them the talents of technology, knowledge and civilisation. In Zeus's opinion, Prometheus cared far too much about humans. When the latter stole fire from the gods and gave it to humans, Zeus was furious. He had Prometheus chained to a rock where his liver was torn out by an eagle (the emblem of Zeus). The liver was seen as the soul, where intelligence also resided (fig. 2). The real torment, however, was the fact that the liver grew back every night, so that Prometheus would have to endure the eagle's brutality for eternity. Did Prometheus regret his actions? No. In political terms, you could call him a dove and Zeus a hawk: the peacemaker versus the warmonger (a parallel between these two birds, familiar from US politics but, in fact, centuries old). Eventually it was Zeus's son Heracles who freed Prometheus from his chains, with Zeus accepting this intervention.

Various cultures have stories that tell of mythical birds. We are familiar with the phoenix from ancient Egypt (and possibly elsewhere in Africa before that). The phoenix was reborn among the Greeks and Romans before reappearing, after many lives (and deaths) in the *Harry Potter* books. In classical antiquity, the phoenix is described as a bird of which there is only one specimen. When its end approaches, it ignites its fragrant nest made of myrrh and incense branches,

FIG. 3
Jacob van Maerlant, *Phoenix*.
Miniature from *Der naturen bloeme*, fol. 83v,
c. 1340–1350. Parchment, 50 × 60 mm.
Royal Library, The Hague, KB KA 16.

from which it is then reborn. Depending on the version of the story, the age that the phoenix reaches varies, from a few hundred years to several thousand. No one has ever seen the bird, so no one knows what it looks like, though some ancient authors attributed purple or golden feathers to it.

The phoenix also played a role in Christianity. The early followers of the religion were eager to draw on symbols from the past to reinforce the authenticity, and thus the legitimacy, of the Christian faith. For example, the Cumaean Sibyl, who made prophecies, was said to have announced the coming of Christ. Something similar happens in the book *Physiologus*, which dates from the early centuries of Christianity and can be described as an anthology of animal symbolism. A parallel is made between the already ancient phoenix and Jesus: the bird's rebirth represents the resurrection of Christ.[3] The parallel is also drawn in *Der naturen bloeme* (c. 1340–1350) by Jacob van Maerlant. Like Jesus, the phoenix (fig. 3) rises three days after its death:

> This unique bird is, to the wise listener, the symbol of Christ: the phoenix has no father or mother, and Christ, our dear brother, as a human being, has no father, and as God, has no mother. The phoenix carefully chooses the tree that grows by the spring. That tree is the cross on which our hope is placed, the spring the baptism that cleanses us of our sins. The fragrant wood with which the phoenix makes its fire is the wood of the cross on which Jesus hung, which he blessed many times and ignited with the fire of his love. He prays to his father – who is dearer to him than all the spices in the world – for forgiveness for us. Christ, our phoenix, burned in the fire of love until he turned to ashes. On the third day, he rose again and then ascended into heaven.[4]

In Jewish legend, the phoenix is called Milcham. This bird was the only creature to resist Eve and the temptation to eat the forbidden fruit in paradise. Therefore, God rewarded Milcham: the bird was allowed to live for a thousand years in a walled city. God himself closed the city gates and promised that no one would enter until the end of time. But after a thousand years, when Milcham's time had come, its nest caught fire. All the birds of its lineage died in the fire, but one egg remained. And so Milcham lives on.[5] Unfortunately, it is unclear how the bird can produce new offspring.

In ancient Greece and Rome, the owl was perceived ambivalently. We are familiar with the bird as the personification of Pallas Athena, the Greek goddess of wisdom; the Greeks considered the owl a sacred animal and a bringer of good omens. The Romans didn't adopt this symbolism, however, when they translated the Greek goddess into their own equivalent, Minerva. In Rome, nocturnal creatures were associated with cemeteries and death; with their shrill cries and silent flight, owls were a source of fear to people.

This marble owl (cat. 44, p. 137) from the second century stands proudly with one claw forward, in which it holds a mouse. The Greek inscription on its base translates as: 'Archates Petrios, the fortune teller, predicts the future for four *assēs*.' That is, for four coins, you could have your future predicted by Archates; the statue served as an advertising column. The hood on the owl's head was used to cover its eyes and keep it calm; only when Archates Petrios needed it, did the hood come off and the owl begin to move. The fortune teller would then study the bird's movements and interpret them in the form of a prediction. Owls were used to tell the future on account of their ability to see clearly in the dark.

The fabled Huma is depicted on countless tiles from thirteenth-century Persia (cat. 42, p. 135). As well as rising from its own ashes, this phoenix-like bird has another special characteristic: it is always in motion, never rests and cannot alight on the ground. Sometimes, it is said to have no legs, similar to the mythical Asian bird of paradise. Like the Chinese phoenix Fenghuang, Huma has a male and a female

FIG. 4
Anonymous, *Bilqis, The Queen of Sheba Facing the Hoopoe, Solomon's Messenger*, Savafid dynasty, Iran, c. 1590–1600.
Ink, watercolour and gold on paper, 100 × 195 cm. British Museum, London.

FIG. 5
Ivan Bilibin, *Prince Ivan and the Firebird*, miniature from *The Firebird*, St. Petersburg, 1901. Colour lithograph. Bibliothèque du musée des Arts Décoratifs, Paris.

side. Huma also appears in poems. It is described as a creature that brings a euphoric sense of happiness if you come across it, touch it or manage to catch it.

Huma also appears in the Islamic work *Manṭiq-uṭ-Ṭayr,* written around 1177 by the Persian Sufi poet Farid ud-Din Attar and translated as *The Conference of the Birds*. It is not Huma who plays the leading role in this work, but Simorgh, whose name means '30 birds'. This play on words is important in the poem. The story can be summed up briefly. The birds of the world gather to search for Simorgh, who is to be their king. As in a frame story, the birds get to know themselves in the course of the quest. Each bird has a reason not to go; Huma, for example, fears that he will lose his privilege to grant kingship if he flies over someone. Ultimately, the birds, having overcome their personal objections, set off on their journey. They must cross a desert and then seven valleys: those of the Quest, Love, Knowledge, Detachment, Unity, Wonderment, and Poverty and Annihilation. Finally, only 30 birds reach the abode of Simorgh. When they see Simorgh appear, they perceive their own reflections in its mirror-like face – hence the pun on the name and the '30 birds'. The hoopoe is the initiator of the journey. This is striking, because this bird appears in the Qur'an not only as the animal that sought land after the flood (the equivalent of the dove sent out by Noah after the Flood in the Bible and the Torah), but also as the messenger of the good and faithful King Solomon, who wants to subjugate the unbelieving or pagan Queen of Sheba (fig. 4).[6]

Another bird known from Islam is Roc (although Dutch readers will be more familiar with it from the Efteling theme park). Roc is a gigantic beast, so large that its parents feed it elephants; the real elephant bird (*Aepyornis maximus*), which once lived in Madagascar, may have been the basis for the stories about Roc. The giant bird appears during the second voyage of Sinbad the Sailor from *One Thousand and One Nights*, when he accidentally ends up in a valley whose floor is strewn with diamonds. Roc is there, fighting a number of snakes. Sinbad, in a state of total panic, sees men throwing chunks of meat from the rock face above. They're hoping that the diamonds will stick to the meat, which Roc will then carry to its nest, where they hope to get their hands on the gems. Sinbad sees through their plan and ties a piece of meat to his back. Not long after, he vanishes into the air in Roc's claws. After a stopover in the nest, he ultimately ends up in Baghdad, rich beyond measure thanks to the diamonds he managed to grab. Later, Sinbad and his crew will have to deal with Roc again – or rather, with a Roc egg (fig. 6).

And then there is the firebird, with its yellow-orange-red feathers. Although sometimes confused with the phoenix, this is another mythical creature that originated in Russia and Slavic cultures (fig. 5). Whereas the phoenix is consumed by fire at the end of its life, the firebird burns throughout its life. Anyone who touches its feathers or tries to catch it is tempting fate, as the bird will change their destiny – and then who knows how things will end. The firebird inspired a ballet of the same name in the early twentieth century for Diaghilev's Ballets Russes, with a score by a young Igor Stravinsky.

FIG. 6
William Frederick Measom, *Les marchands cassèrent l'œuf* (The Merchants Broke the Egg), 1865. Engraving from Gustave Doré, *Les Mille et une Nuits*, 200 × 290 mm, col. 1, p. 147. Bibliothèque nationale de France, Paris.

Elsewhere in this book, we encounter the dove as a metaphor for love. But there is more to say about this bird. Jews and Christians are acquainted with the story of Noah, who released a dove after the Flood to search for dry land. When the bird returned with an olive branch in its beak, it was a sign that land was near. Christians came to see the dove as the embodiment of the soul and the Holy Spirit. The dove appears at three key moments in Christianity and/or Christian iconography. First, when the bird announces to Mary that she will conceive and bear Jesus. Years later, when Jesus is baptised in the River Jordan, a dove descends upon him and a voice from heaven declares that he is God's beloved son. This moment marks the joint presence of the Trinity: the Father (God in heaven), the Son (Jesus) and the Holy Spirit (in the form of the dove). Finally, there is Pentecost, a feast day on which Christians commemorate the descent of the Holy Spirit. In *Triptych with the Descent of the Holy Spirit, the Ascension of Christ, and the Assumption of Mary* (cat. 40, pp. 132–133) by Lucas van Leyden (1489–1533), the middle panel shows the Holy Spirit – again in the form of a dove – giving the disciples their divine task, namely, to travel and share their stories about Jesus with the world. This is the actual beginning of the Christian Church, ten days after Jesus ascended to heaven, as seen on the left panel.

Meaning has also been attributed in Christianity to the pelican and to the goldfinch; in both cases, these stories revolve around blood. The pelican mother was said to peck open her own breast with her beak and feed her young with the blood flowing from the wound (fig. 7). She thus sacrificed herself out of love for her little ones. Although a compelling story about mercy and altruism, associated with Jesus's own sacrifice, this doesn't, of course, make it true. During the breeding season, a red spot appears on the chest of some pelicans, which was apparently seen as blood. Pelicans collect food for their young in their beaks, press it against their chest and then feed their young.[7]

FIG. 7
Pelican Piercing its own Breast (detail). Miniature from *Bestiarius*, fol. 32r, 15th century. Parchment, 252 × 180 mm. Huis van het Boek, The Hague, 10 B 25.

Sometimes, sacred connections are even easier to make, as in the case of the African jacana (family *Jacanidae*), nicknamed the Jesus bird. Because of its elongated toes, which allow it to move easily on floating vegetation, it seems as if it is, like Jesus, actually walking on water.

And why are there golden weathercocks on church towers? Because it is a crowing cockerel that awakens the faithful, just as church bells call them to church. But also because the cockerel was once adopted by the Church as a pre-Christian symbol to relate the animal to the story of Jesus's betrayal. 'Before the cock crow, thou shalt deny me thrice,' Jesus said to the apostle Peter. And so it came to pass: Peter betrayed Jesus three times out of fear of being arrested. After his third denial, he heard a cock crow and remembered Jesus's prediction. Remorse and shame followed, but Peter continued to preach the teachings of Christ throughout his life.

What about the birds in the Garden of Eden, or paradise? Peter Paul Rubens (1577–1640) and Jan Brueghel the Elder (1568–1625) painted a large number of them in *The Garden of Eden with the Fall of Man* (fig. 8), which dates from around 1615 and is in the collection of the Mauritshuis. Most striking in this picture are the exotic birds. 'The more colourful, the better', is what Vasco da Gama, Columbus, Magellan, Cortés and many other explorers and colonisers after them must have thought when they transported parrots, parakeets, macaws, birds of paradise, marabou storks and cockatoos from Africa, Asia and the Americas to the capitals of Europe. Merchant ships in the Netherlands had already been sailing to Asia and the Americas for some 20 years, but the supply of exotic animals to Europe had been going on for much longer. In Rubens and Brueghel's painting of Eden, we see an ostrich, peacocks, parrots, parakeets and toucans. Naturally, birds of paradise could not be missing either. Strikingly, Brueghel, who painted all the animals except the snake and horse, depicted the bird of paradise standing at Adam's feet. Until then, birds of paradise had been painted without legs, based on the earlier belief that these animals only ever flew and never alighted. Fauna experts in Europe were led to believe that birds of paradise were legless simply because the legs were removed from the bird skins prepared by the Indigenous inhabitants of New Guinea.

In a recent study, art historian Paul Smith has shown that all the animals depicted in *The Garden of Eden with the Fall of Man* express the peaceful atmosphere of paradise: after their expulsion from Eden, a songbird would never again perch so nonchalantly on a branch next to a hawk. But the birds also have meanings in their own right. Some as individuals: the peacock represents temptation, the heron brings good luck, and the bird of paradise bears its metaphorical meaning in its name. Other animals have a clear meaning as a pair, such as the green birds with red heads between Adam and Eve. Known colloquially as lovebirds, their scientific

FIG. 8
Jan Brueghel the Elder and Peter Paul Rubens, *The Garden of Eden with the Fall of Man*, c. 1615. Oil on panel, 74.3 × 114.7 cm. Mauritshuis, The Hague.

name is *Agapornis* – in Greek, *agape* means love and *ornis* bird. Brueghel placed some avian pairs together, but most of the males and females are separated, making the painting a wonderful picture puzzle. See if you can spot the partners of the blue-and-yellow macaw, the white-throated toucan, the hoopoe, the great spotted woodpecker, the magpie and the bird of paradise.

Let's return briefly to the time of the pharaohs in Egypt, where the ibis also played a divine role. The African sacred ibis, also known as the Nile bird, was revered as the personification of the god Thoth, the inventor of writing, civilisation and the moon. This is why the bird is called 'sacred'. Thoth was usually depicted as a man with the head of an ibis. The bird's curved beak has been associated with the shape of a waxing moon. Ibises were sacrificed in huge numbers, mummified and buried, like the falcon. The bird is predominantly white with black legs, neck, head and wing tips. The description of the ibis in Jacob van Maerlant's *Der naturen bloeme* is rather amusing:

> All ibises are white, except those in the Egyptian city of Pelusium, which are black. Some people think the ibis and the stork are the same bird, but that is not the case, unless one wants to consider ibises as a type of stork, which no one can imagine because they have never been seen in Europe. Pliny mentions that ibises have a curved beak, while storks have a straight beak.[8]

In Brazil, the scarlet or red ibis provided the feathers used by Indigenous populations to make ceremonial cloaks that were considered sacred (fig. 9). In the posthumous portrait of the English princess Mary Stuart (wife of William II of Orange) by Adriaen Hanneman (1603–1671), which hangs in the Mauritshuis, Mary is wearing a cloak made of red ibis feathers. Was she going to a fancy-dress ball, unaware of the significance of the sacred garment she had on? The cloak was most likely brought to the Netherlands by Johan Maurits, founder of the Mauritshuis, who was governor of the Dutch West India Company's colony Dutch Brazil from 1636 to 1644. Maurits was found guilty of smuggling enslaved people for

FIG. 9
Tupinamba cloak. Plant material, feathers, 120 cm long. Museo Nacional, Rio de Janeiro, Brazil.

his own gain, and was dismissed by the company.[9] This forced him to sell all the paintings and other objects he had brought with him from Brazil. King Frederik III of Denmark acquired the works of the painter Albert Eckhout and several Brazilian cloaks made of ibis feathers. When the National Museum of Brazil in Rio de Janeiro lost its entire collection of such cloaks in a fire in 2018, Denmark returned one of its cloaks to its country of origin, where it was ceremonially received by the Tupinambá people in 2024.[10]

In 2024, the Indigenous Brazilian artist Daiara Tukano created a mural for the Mauritshuis (cat. 41, p. 134) that builds a bridge between the present and the seventeenth century, when Johan Maurits ruled the colony of Dutch Brazil. The mural, entitled *Wirõ ah'cipá* (Shimmers of the Wind), features several graceful blue swallows in flight. These birds, which are beloved in both Brazil and Europe, here carry a special message. The first barn swallow was a joyful sign of spring for ancient Germanic peoples. In the nineteenth and twentieth centuries, the sighting of the first swallow in our regions was announced in news bulletins and people would drink to its arrival. Not only was the bird itself welcomed, but also its nest, as it was said to protect houses and farms from lightning and fire. If you killed a swallow, you could expect terrible hardship. Daiara Tukano sees the swallow as a creature that, given its long migratory flight from continent to continent, symbolises absolute freedom. She contrasts it with Carel Fabritius's *Goldfinch*, which lives in captivity. She chose this painting as the starting point for her mural. Tukano said the following about it:

> Carel Fabritius's *Goldfinch* immediately caught my eye and stuck in my mind. A little bird chained up. The idea of a bird being unable to fly because it is all chained up made me feel very uncomfortable. For us Yé'pá Mahsã people, birds are very sacred, and it is important for them to be free. They are messengers who go through different layers of the world.[11]

1 Riclefs 2022.
2 *The Guardian* 2024.
3 Verduin n.d.
4 Translation by Patrick Lennon of Van Maerlant 1995.
5 *Beleven* n.d.
6 *My articles* 2022.
7 Mulders 2021, p. 31.
8 Translation by Patrick Lennon of Van Maerlant 1995.
9 For more on the life and times of Johan Maurits, see the Mauritshuis website: https://www.mauritshuis.nl/en/what-s-on/exhibitions/johan-maurits-and-the-mauritshuis#governor.
10 *The Art Newspaper* n.d.
11 *Mauritshuis* n.d.

Cat. 38

Peter Paul Rubens, 'Modello' for the *Ascension of the Virgin*, c. 1622–1625. Oil on panel, 87.8 × 59.1 cm. Mauritshuis, The Hague, purchased with the support of the Friends of the Mauritshuis Foundation, 1956, inv. no. 926.

Cat. 39

Workshop of Dieric Bouts, *Virgin and Child Seated on a Turf Bench*, c. 1450.
Oil on panel, 41.2 × 29.6 cm. Enschede, Rijksmuseum Twenthe,
Enschede, inv. no. 0046.

Cat. 40

Circle of Lucas van Leyden, *Triptych with the Descent of the Holy Spirit, the Ascension of Christ, and the Assumption of Mary*, 1525–1549. Oil on panel, 65.5 × 84.5 cm. Museum Catherijneconvent, Utrecht, inv. no. ABM s114.

Cat. 41

Daiara Tukano, *Wirõ ah'cipá* (Shimmers of the Wind), 2024.
Mauritshuis, The Hague.

Cat. 42

Anonymous, Star-shaped tile with an inscription and a bird, Kashan, c. 1290–1311. Ceramic, 20.3 cm. (diam.) Rijksmuseum, Amsterdam, inv. no. BK-1992-38.

Cat. 43

Mummified falcon, Egypt and Nubia, 304–30 BCE.
Organic material, linen, stucco, polychromy, 52 × 9.5 × 8.1 cm.
Rijksmuseum van Oudheden, Leiden, inv. no. F 1975/11.3.

Cat. 44

Anonymous, Owl of Thoms, Mediterranean,
2nd century. Marble, 77 × 20 × 18 cm.
Rijksmuseum van Oudheden, Leiden, inv. no. ZM-7.

Cat. 45

Pendant in the shape of a soulbird, Egypt and Nubia, 332 BCE–395. Metal and gold, 2.2 × 3.7 cm. Rijksmuseum van Oudheden, Leiden, inv. no. L.V.63-m.3.

Cat. 46

Statue of a ba bird, Egypt, 700–332 BCE. Wood, 15.5 × 4.8 cm. Rijksmuseum van Oudheden, Leiden, inv. no. L.IX.30.

Cat. 47

Henri Cartier-Bresson, *Henri Matisse in His Studio (Vence)*, 1944. Gelatin silver print, 23.7 × 35.8 cm. Fondation Cartier-Bresson, Paris, inv. no. HCB1951007W00965/14C//1.

Cat. 48

Pablo Picasso, *La colombe* (The Dove), 1949.
Lithography on zinc, 546 × 691 mm. Picasso Museum – Die Sammlung Huizinga, Münster, inv. no. GR 443 | 141.

Lovebirds

Martine Gosselink

Human languages contain many bird-related words associated with love or sex. English alone has several. For example, 'bird' or 'birdie' is a derogatory (and now rather old-fashioned) slang term in British English for a young woman or girlfriend. Girls have been referred to as 'chicks' since the early twentieth century. It was considered offensive, as if young women were delicate, fluffy creatures. The use of the word was particularly criticised at the height of the women's liberation movement in the 1970s. But nothing is as changeable as language, and soon after new life was deliberately breathed into the term, this time by women themselves. The phrase 'chicks rule!' and terms such as 'chick lit', 'chick flick' and 'chick culture' have been commonly used ever since and are now largely free from any negative connotation.

In Dutch, the phrase *lekker kippetje* (tasty-looking chick) is used to describe a girl's (erotic) appeal. In French, the word *coq* means rooster, like the Middle English *coc.* The Middle Dutch *cocke* means male bird. Since 1450, the word 'cock' has also been used in English as a slang term for the penis.[1] The Dutch term *duifje* (little dove) has been employed as a girl's name or as a pet name for a loved one since the seventeenth century. We often refer to a couple in the first weeks of their relationship, when they cannot keep their hands off each other, as a pair of *tortelduiven* – in English, 'turtle doves'; in other words, lovebirds. Nowadays, if you say to a friend in Dutch, *Zullen we gaan vogelen?,* it means that we want to go birdwatching. In the seventeenth century, however, such a question would have raised eyebrows or reddened cheeks since, at that time, *vogelen* meant having sex or cheating on one's partner.

Have a look at the engraving by Gillis van Breen (c. 1560–after 1602) (fig. 1). A woman is gesturing towards a man's basket. In it is a live rooster, with a dead duck on top. The rhyme below the engraving reads:

> How much for this bird, bird-catcher?
> It has been sold, right?
> To a landlady, whom I *vogel* all year long.

The woman can't buy the bird, because it has already been sold to someone else, someone whom the man has been supplying with birds all year long – that is, with whom he has been having sex. The fact that the man is groping his crotch further underlines his words.

Against this background, it is not difficult to imagine the message conveyed in *The Useless Moral Lesson* by Godfried Schalcken (1643–1706) (cat. 51, p. 149). A young woman is about to let her little bird – virginity – escape from the box. The elderly lady next to her can warn her all she wants, but she is anything but receptive to her sermon. We know that

FIG. 1
Gillis van Breen, *Bird Seller*, c. 1595–1610.
Engraving, 185 × 235 mm. Rijksmuseum, Amsterdam.

FIG. 2
Godfried Schalcken, *The Doctor's Examination*, c. 1690. Oil on panel, 35 × 28.6 cm. Mauritshuis, The Hague.

she should have listened, however, thanks to the pendant to this painting, *The Doctor's Examination* (fig. 2), which shows us the young woman in a less fortunate situation. She is pregnant. The doctor, a so-called *piskijker* (a quack, literally a 'piss-looker'), has just announced the not-so-happy news, after looking closely at the irrefutable evidence: in the bottle of urine he holds, we can already see an embryo swimming. Pissed off, the father on the left looks up at his daughter, while her dear brother on the right makes an obscene gesture as he gazes at us knowingly.

What are we to make of the way in which the Leiden painter Arie de Vois (1632–1680) portrayed himself as a nonchalant hunter (cat. 50, p. 148)? Nothing much seems to be happening, you might think. De Voie is sitting at ease with his dog at the foot of a tree. He holds a dead partridge and a hunting rifle upright in his hands. The scene seems innocent, but make no mistake, this is an unvarnished portrait of a man with a powerful sex drive. Hunting symbolises courting and the partridge represents sex. It was claimed that female partridges could be impregnated while flying, simply by getting close to a male. Male partridges were said to destroy the eggs laid by females so that they would not brood and therefore would be available for mating.[2] Now that you know this, you might look at such hunting portraits differently. De Voie was clearly hunting for a partner.

Why are birds so closely associated with love? Is it because they are identified with reproduction, spring, burgeoning new life, finding a mate, building a nest and, invariably, as the Dutch saying goes, *In mei steevast een ei* (In May all birds an egg shall lay)? It is certainly not on account of the idyll of eternal fidelity, because only a handful of birds are monogamous, including swans, cranes, turtle doves, sea eagles and black-tailed godwits. So, yes, the connection between birds and both romantic and carnal love generally has to do with building nests. One of the most beautiful lines of poetry ever composed on this subject is also one of the oldest written sentences in Dutch (cat. 49, p. 147), dating from the eleventh century and one that many Dutch and Flemish children learned at school. Below is the entire line, preceded by the same sentence in Latin.

> *Abent omnes uolucres nidos inceptos nisi ego et*
> *tu quid expectamus nunc.*
> *Hebban olla uogala nestas hagunnan hinase*
> *hic anda thu uuat unbidan uue nu.*

In modern English, this translates as: 'All the birds have begun to build their nests, except you and me; what are we waiting for?' This line is further confirmation that it must be the urge to nest that imposes the parallel between love and birds.

The latest research reveals that this was written by a man, a monk, who wrote these lines in the margin of a manuscript to try out his newly cut goose quill. The language he used may be that of a woman, however, since the text corresponds to songs sung by women at the time.

Of all the associations between birds and love, one in particular has been prevalent since before the Common Era: that of the dove with love, but also with peace. It is the dove, a representation of the Holy Spirit, that 'tells' Mary that she is pregnant. But long before the birth of Christ, the dove was associated with goddesses and other mythical women. The Greek word for dove, *peristera*, was also the name of a nymph in Greek mythology. She intervened when Aphrodite, the goddess of love (Venus in Latin), and her son Eros, the god of love, competed to see who could pick the most flowers. Eros was in the lead until Peristera gave her flowers to Aphrodite, who thus won the contest. An angry Eros turned the nymph into a dove, and the bird became the symbol of Aphrodite (fig. 3). She is often represented by a dove, which is sometimes shown pulling her flower-covered chariot.

The Greeks, for their part, adopted this iconography from the Syrians, who saw the dove as the sacred companion of their goddess of love, Astarte. She in turn is connected to the goddess Ishtar (also known as Inanna), who was worshipped in Mesopotamia (4000–539 BCE) and whom we know from the ancient epic *Gilgamesh*. Ishtar is also associated with beauty, sensuality, romance and reproduction. Since the Bronze Age, the dove has been linked to divine women who symbolise love and reproduction, from Ishtar to Mary. But why the dove – or the pigeon, as it tends to be called in urban settings – which are ubiquitous in our cities and generally unloved? They poo everywhere and are nicknamed 'flying rats'. Office buildings and shops are widely equipped with bird spikes to prevent them from nesting. So why was this very animal chosen as the symbol of love?

There is an unexpected reason for this. We know that Roman medicine and traditional Chinese health sciences associated bile (in humans) with anger and malign temperaments. This is where the term 'black bile' comes from, which can be traced back to the theory of humours of Claudius Galenus, better known as Galen. This Graeco-Roman physician translated the four humours – blood, yellow bile, black bile, phlegm – into personality types. What did he find? That doves do not have a gall bladder (which stores bile). Hence the assumption that this bird does not have any bad or negative emotions, which is why it came to symbolise gentleness. Add to these traits the pleasant cooing sounds that the males use to seduce females, and there you have it.

Finally, there are turtle doves, which, unlike ordinary doves or pigeons, mate for life. They show their love by cooing softly to each other. They also brood throughout the year, with the male and female taking turns to sit on the eggs. Have you ever seen a male turtle dove perform its impressive mating flight for its female? It is performed so lovingly that you immediately understand why the turtle dove beats the 'ordinary' peace dove and represents unconditional love.

Many other birds are associated with love. Think of the story of Leda and the swan (cat. 52, pp. 150–151). Although, can we really speak of love? This is, rather, a case of brute force and rape. The swan was actually Zeus, king of the gods. He wanted Leda, Queen of Sparta, but she turned him down. Zeus therefore took the form of a swan, a creature that would not arouse her suspicion if he approached her. When he had come close to her, the swan overpowered Leda and impregnated her. The children she bore hatched from an egg.

Peace, love, sex and birds – all one and the same, according to the bird diviners of antiquity (fig. 4). They interpreted bird behaviour as clues to the future, including future loves and partners. What species of bird they saw, how many there were, how they sang, moved and flew – everything mattered. Our word 'auspices' (omen, supervision, protection) is derived from this practice: *avis* means 'bird' and *spicere* means 'to see'. No political decision was made without the advice of the augurs, as these diviners were called. At a certain point, a distinction arose between official and private augurs. The latter studied birds to predict the quality of proposed marriages. Even today, the sighting of a particular bird is still seen as an omen. Nothing new under the sun there.

However old the connection between birds, love and sex may be, it remains impossible to say exactly why birds, their feathers and their flight were sexualised or associated with love by humans. One of the earliest texts to do so is the Song of Solomon (1:15), which we are familiar with from the Tanakh and the Bible and which dates from the sixth to second century BCE. It reads: 'Behold, thou art fair, my love; behold, thou art fair; thou hast doves' eyes.'

FIG. 4
Phersu with birds, 530–520 BCE. Fresco in the Tomb of the Augurs, Monterozzi necropolis, Tarquinia.

FIG. 3
Limestone figurine of a dove, Cyprus, c. 600–480 BCE. The Metropolitan Museum of Art, New York.

1 Dalzell and Victor 2015, pp. 275–280.
2 Boussauw 2024, pp. 83–84.

Cat. 49

Ælfric, Abbot of Eynsham, 'Hebban olla uogala' ('Have all birds begun their nests?'), c. 1000–1050. Parchment, 315 × 220 mm. Poem from *Homilies in Old English*, fol. 169v. Bodleian Libraries, Oxford, Bodl. 340.

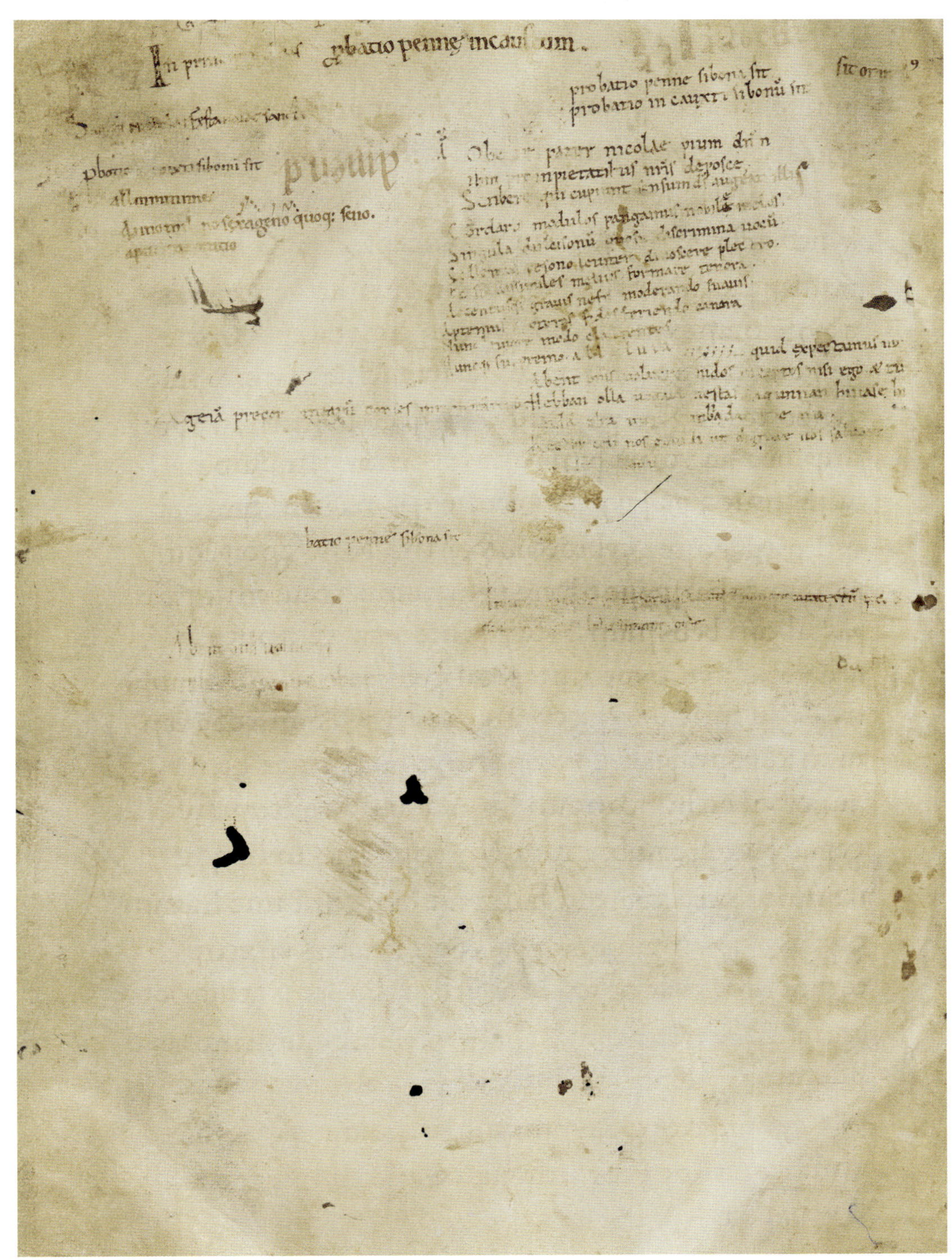

Cat. 50

Arie de Vois, *Self-Portrait as a Hunter*, c. 1660. Oil on panel, 28.7 × 21.8 cm. Mauritshuis, The Hague, inv. no. 204.

Cat. 51

Godfried Schalcken, *The Useless Moral Lesson*, c. 1690. Oil on panel, 34.8 × 28.1 cm. Mauritshuis, The Hague, inv. no. 160.

MICHAEL
ANGELVS
Formosa hæc Læda est, cignus fit Iuppiter illam
Comprimit, hoc geminum quis credat parturit ouum,

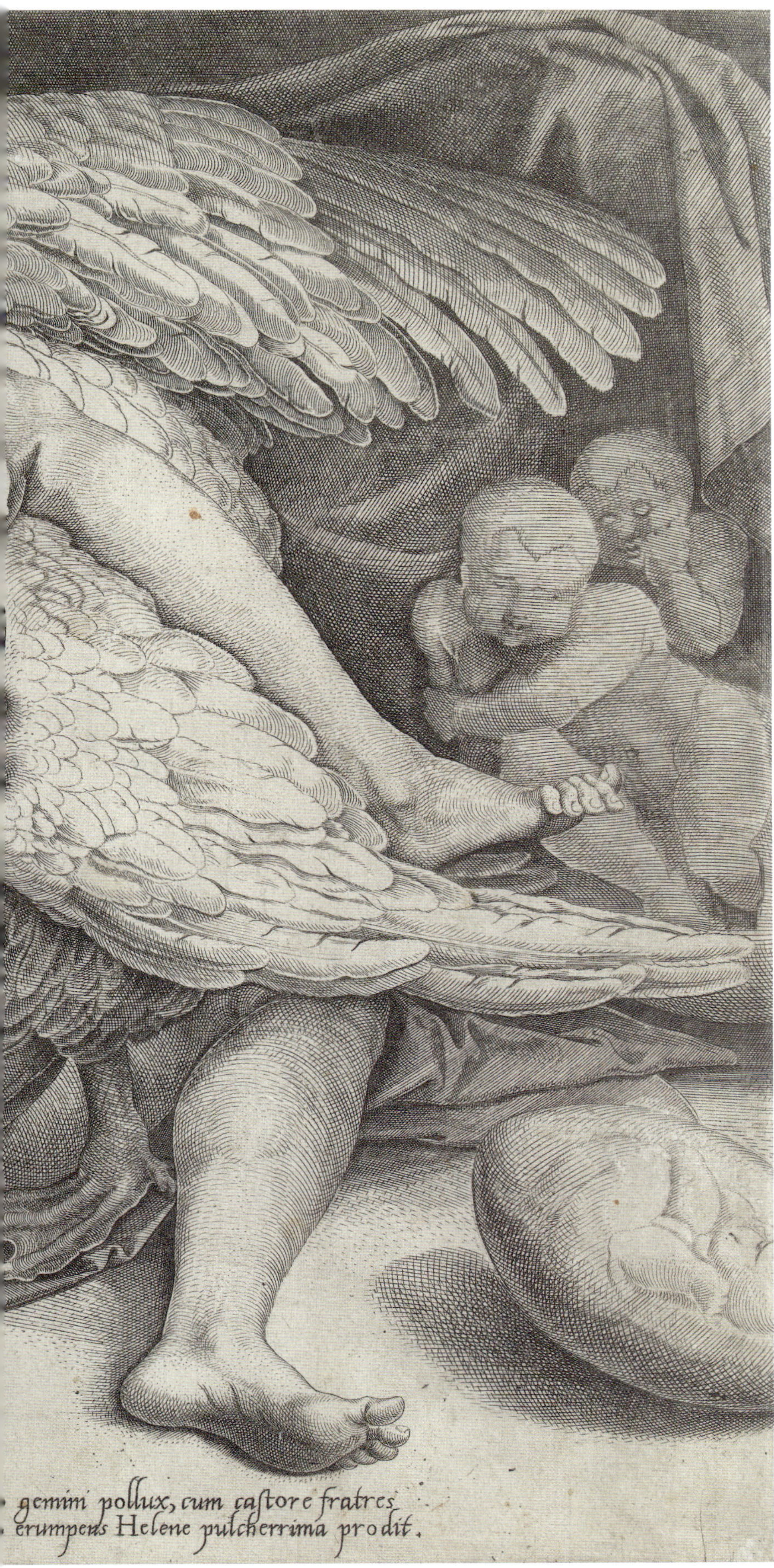

Cat. 52

Cornelis Bos after Michelangelo Buonarotti,
Leda and the Swan, c. 1544–1545.
Engraving, 302 × 410 mm. Rijksmuseum,
Amsterdam, inv. no. RP-P-BI-2758.

Cat. 53

Tracey Emin, *You Saved Me*, 2014. Bronze, 31.5 × 51 × 34 cm.
Studio Tracey Emin, courtesy White Cube Gallery, London, inv. no. TE5240.

Lovebirds

Cat. 54

Louise Lawler, *Birdcalls*, 1972–1981. Audio recording and text, 7 min 1 sec. LeWitt Collection, Chester.

Cat. 55

Leonora Carrington, *Señor Ruiz, el Ruiseñor* (Señor Ruiz, the Nightingale), 1967. Gouache, c. 104 × 71 cm. Collection Betty and Homero Aridjis, Mexico.

Portrait, 1982.

Señor Ruiz
el Ruiseñor
LEONORA CARRINGTON
1967

Bird Artists

Eva Meijer

FIG. 1
Nest, made by crows in Landsmeer.

FIG. 2
Bird's nest, maker unknown.

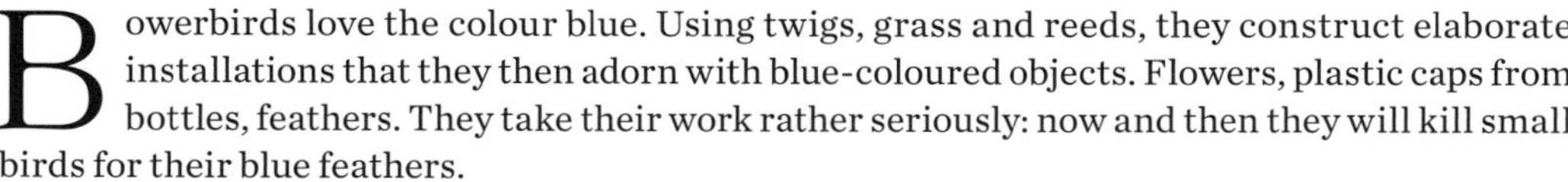

Bowerbirds love the colour blue. Using twigs, grass and reeds, they construct elaborate installations that they then adorn with blue-coloured objects. Flowers, plastic caps from bottles, feathers. They take their work rather seriously: now and then they will kill small birds for their blue feathers.

Bowerbirds are not the only birds that make intricate sculptures. Weaver birds weave nests from grass and other plants. The cocoon-shaped family nests are fairly well known, but they also create larger objects. Sociable weavers build colonies counting many rooms that can house up to a hundred pairs of birds. Even more common nests, like those of blackbirds, tits and crows, are not only functional but also beautiful (figs. 1 and 2).

FIG. 3
Rooster in Knockvologan, Isle of Mull, Scotland.

Birds express their creativity not just by building nests. They sing to communicate with each other, to warn others and to attract mates. It is not only the message that is important, but also how it is conveyed. Their song is determined by the species they belong to, but their character is also of significance. In her books, bird researcher Len Howard described in detail how different great tits sing and what they say to each other. Some birds can do even more with their voices. Earlier this year, I was staying in Australia and one morning I heard gunshots coming from the bushes. Not real gunshots, but shots as in a computer game. It turned out to be lyrebirds, who are known for imitating human sounds, including the chainsaws used to cut down the trees that make up their habitat. Apparently, this sound interested them. The birds also build platforms to perch on for extra effect (fig. 3).

Dancing is another way birds express themselves. Once they reach the age of five, albatrosses meet several potential mates every year at a fixed location where they dance together. Year after year, they refine their dance – with movements, calls, looks, pointing and pecking each other's feathers. With every year that goes by, a number of dance partners drop out until, after three or four years, the one true partner is left. Once paired up, they stay together for the rest of their lives. When they see each other again after being separated, they dance their own dance.

BIRDS ARE ALSO INDIVIDUALS

Humans in Western cultures like to believe that they are radically different in terms of language, music and art from other animals, such as birds. But such a view is no longer tenable. Research by ethologists and biologists has shown that crows, for example, possess 'theory of mind' (meaning that they anticipate what others will do, which shows in turn that they know that others also think), great tits have cultures, and ravens master complex languages, though we understand little of them. Chickens talk to their chicks while still in the egg, and chicks are better at arithmetic than human babies.

FIG. 4
Gathering of cormorants on the Amstel River.

Humans are not superior to other animals: different creatures give meaning to their existence in their own way. Nor does a boundary run between our lives: we influence one another. Think of the starlings at Rotterdam Central Station that mimic the beeping of the Sprinter train, misleading travellers. Think also of Olivier Messiaen, the famous composer inspired by birdsong; and Kate Bush, who opened her album *Aerial* with the call of a wood pigeon. White cockatoos in Sydney have figured out how to open rubbish bins (each different group has its own technique), forcing humans to play catch-up as they keep having to adapt the bins. There are even parrots in Australia that, having escaped or been released, teach their fellow parrots human language (English) as a second language.

BIRDS AS ARTISTS

As this exhibition shows, birds have been capturing our imagination for centuries. Birds have helped to shape art history, both through the pictures we have made of them and the materials we have taken from them – egg in paint, feathers in masks. In general, however, their agency as creators is not explicitly recognised. Works of art often repeat existing assumptions about non-human animals – birds long for freedom, dogs are loyal. More often still, art about animals is not about animals at all, but uses them only as a metaphor to say something about humans. This confirms an image of birds as simple creatures that act solely on instinct, and of humans as the chosen species. This is regrettable, since it is art itself that can help us to conceive and try out new relations. That is why it is time we saw birds – and other non-human animals – as artists.

The question of whether animals are artists is as much a question about 'animals' – what they are, what non-human animals think and are capable of – as it is one about what art is. It is also a question about who has the final say in that matter. As Jacques Derrida wrote, the term 'animals' is problematic, especially when contrasted with 'humans'. Humans are also animals, and if you gather all other animals in a single group through language, you are not doing justice to the differences that exist between them. The term 'animals' also legitimises the exploitation of real animals – after all, they are just animals. The word 'bird' is just as vague and arbitrary. Humans classify certain other animals in this way, but a bird does not consider itself a bird. Even though they may inhabit the same garden, a chicken and a great tit have little in common. And in this case too, language distinguishes two groups: humans on one side, birds on the other – while, in fact, all kinds of possible relations exist between creatures from these groups, and all kinds of differences.

The question of aesthetic awareness in birds and of their creative ability is often linked to certain cognitive capacities. Such as the ability to reflect on one's actions and work according to a predetermined plan. But like humans, birds at times reflect on their actions and at times act spontaneously. Moreover, we still do not know much about what birds think and want because, as the philosopher Vinciane Despret has written, we have never asked animals the right questions. Moreover, art is precisely a practice that appeals not only to the intellect, but also to the emotions and power of imagination of both viewer and creator.

This brings us to the question of what art actually is. One of the interesting and amusing characteristics of art is that artists have asked this question over and over again in the course of time. Paintings and sculptures are art, but actions and thoughts can also be art. Think of feminist performance art, conceptual art and walking art. Nowadays, collectives are popular, challenging the clichéd image of the artist as an individual (male) genius and highlighting the fact that we are always dependent on others, including in the creation of art. Art can have all kinds of functions in culture and social relations. Ultimately, it is a practice that provides meaning.

It is the same for birds. For the nest builders, the singers, the dancers. Their work is not the same as human art. It sometimes resembles it, as in the case of the bowerbirds or the compositions of the lyrebirds, as composer Hollis Taylor has demonstrated. But nests combine aesthetic insight with functionality in a way than differs from what we know. Perhaps we need a new term for this intertwining of art and design (fig. 5).

FIG. 5
Heron on a work by Jan Goossen near Gaasperplas metro station, Amsterdam.

FIG. 6
Pigeon's nest at Maashaven metro station, Rotterdam.

Understanding others begins with paying attention. Therefore, I wish to invite you, during this exhibition, to search for the real birds that made it possible, and to bear that view in mind when you leave (fig. 6). In an age of far-right governments, arms races and climate emergencies, it may seem frivolous to listen to the song of blackbirds or learn about the culture of jackdaws. But, as humans, we need to rethink our attitude. For ourselves, in order to survive in a time of eco-political crises. And for others, including birds. Humans are destroying their habitats, bird species are dying out on a large scale, insects are disappearing, making life difficult for birds, and the Earth is warming up, forcing a great many animals to leave their habitats. Humans also keep them captive, as companions or for food.

Sometimes they are exploited on an extreme scale, as in the case of chickens, turkeys and pigeons. Chickens are seen as the characteristic species of the Anthropocene, the age of humans. They also characterise the Capitalocene, the age of capitalism. In the future, our art will pale in comparison with the bones of billions of birds. And those bones were once living creatures who knew only suffering in their short lives.

The world is more beautiful when you look at and listen to other animals. But ultimately, what matters is that they too have only one life, which is the most important thing to them – and we must respect that. Birds do not belong to human beings. Birds belong only to the air and to themselves (fig. 7).

FIG. 7
Flying jackdaws.

Birds of a Feather

Laura Cumming

FIG. 1
Jan Weenix, *Dead Swan*, c. 1700–1719. Oil on canvas, 245.5 × 294 cm. Mauritshuis, The Hague. on long-term loan to Rijksmuseum Twenthe, Enschede.

Hope is the thing with feathers -
That perches in the soul -
And sings the tune without the words -
And never stops - at all –

EMILY DICKINSON

Hope is a bird that never stays still. It darts about inside the human soul like a lark in the sky, surging upwards without cause, singing songs without knowing any words, sustained only by its buoyant lifting wings. A bird is hope embodied and the spirit of so much more. But it is also a form of daily magic. Birds have the power to leave the earth at will, rising high above us, hovering and landing wherever they wish, in treetops, on waves, far across the ocean on some other continent. They appear, and vanish, so mysteriously that our language has no adequate words for their unparalleled performance – swooping and diving, circling and gliding, fluttering, soaring, wheeling and disappearing into the blue. How to keep such a non-stop creature still: how to draw a bird, when stillness is against its nature?

The easiest way, alas, is simply to kill it. This is the mode of still life, or *nature morte* as art history mordantly calls it. Seventeenth-century Dutch art, with its infinity of sub-specialisations in every genre, has many masters of the stone-dead bird, laid out on a ledge with flowers or fruit or other once-vital creatures. Jan Weenix found fame with the most exotic birds he could acquire, shot by hunters outside his native Amsterdam. He started out with cockerel, guinea fowl and partridge, moved on to brilliant turquoise kingfishers, positioned for eye-catching effect in the foreground of these pile-ups of avian corpses, but he is most renowned for his paintings of dead swans (fig. 1).

Weenix painted many swans, each commission a boast for its wealthy owner, for it was a restricted privilege to be allowed to hunt these large birds. Nobody quite knows when the Mauritshuis masterpiece was painted, though Weenix was probably in his late sixties or seventies. Decades of study are condensed in this vision of the spreadeagled swan: the shine on its immense articulated wing, the opalescent whiteness of the breast, running from pearl to gold, the soft underside of the tail. Weenix paints what we could never see: not just the breast, but the legs that keep the water ballet afloat. For this noble bird is hung up by one foot, in order to display its majesty at full length. The neck becomes a limb, gracefully descending towards the cruel butt of a gun. Weenix adds a smaller corpse for scale, a finch the length of the swan's beak. The sight is frightful, unnatural: a stately bird rifled. The finch is given more dignity.

Yet this is also a painting of awestruck knowledge. What are they, these creatures, two-limbed like us and yet nothing like us at all. Diogenes is said to have mocked Plato's definition of man as a featherless biped by turning up with a plucked chicken: 'Here is Plato's Man.' For many artists, the difference is so obviously the miracle of flight that the wings become paramount. Leonardo scrutinises the anatomy of bone and ligature to try to understand the mechanism of bird flight in his drawings (cat. 32, p. 110). Dürer's watercolour of the rainbow glory of a European blue roller's wing is equal, in all its astoundingly beautiful particularity, to the serried pennants of the wing itself (fig. 1, p. 106).

These birds are by definition dead, their wings laid out, their legs examined for backward-moving joints. The famous French-American birdman, John James Audubon, went so far as to kill and eat most of the thousands of species he painted, from bald eagles to snowy owls and even that preternaturally still bird, the heron, while travelling the continent with gun and brush. His *American Flamingo* (fig. 4), from *The Birds of America*, is an adult male spotted as Audubon passed through the Florida Keys. He captures something of its bizarre anatomy – the long twisty neck, disproportionately large bill and stick legs, the brilliant pink that will eventually turn scarlet. But the bird is subjugated to the design; perfect for what would become Audubon's most popular poster.

FIG. 2
John James Audubon, *California Condor*, 1827–1838. Hand-coloured aquatint from *The Birds of America*, vol. 5, plate 426. Teylers Museum, Haarlem.

FIG. 3
John James Audubon, *Burrowing Owl, Large-Headed Burrowing Owl, Little Night Owl, Columbian Owl and Short-cared Owl*, 1827–1838. Hand-coloured aquatint from *The Birds of America*, vol. 5, plate 432. Teylers Museum, Haarlem.

FIG. 4 (Cat. 6, p. 67)
John James Audubon, *American Flamingo*, 1827–1838. Hand-coloured aquatint from *The Birds of America*, vol. 5, plate 432. Teylers Museum, Haarlem.

There is a staggering photograph in this show, by Henri Cartier-Bresson, of a bird keeping still for an artist. The elderly Matisse holds a white dove in one hand while sketching it with the other. The bird does not seem to flinch. Three more doves sit on top of a cage, unconfined, as sunlight streams through the studio window. Matisse, quick as a bird, will soon return this dove to its freedom (cat. 47, p. 140).

Matisse allowed birds to fly all around his house in the South of France. They flitter through his later cut-outs. His studio assistant recalled that it was the shape of a bird that first inspired this innovation: 'Matisse had cut out a swallow from a sheet of writing paper and, as it distressed him to tear up this beautiful shape and throw it away, he put it up on this wall ... Over the following weeks other shapes were cut out and put up.'

Matisse gave his last doves to his old rival Picasso: 'They look like some you have already painted.' Sure enough, a biblical white dove was Picasso's symbol of peace for the poster for the 1949 Paris World Peace Conference. You might say it has even become Pablo's own emblem (fig. 16, p. 29).

But that dove, like so many birds in art, is a flight of fantasy – or at very least a feat of memory. For though we now have shutter speeds so rapid as to catch the millisecond beat of a violet-tailed hummingbird's wings, almost everything drawn or painted or sculpted across the millennia must originate with a recollection.

It is true that some birds can sit still all day, especially birds of prey, leaving their perch only once for a kill. A peregrine spent almost a whole winter waiting motionless on the top of London's Tate Modern, where several artists were able to draw it. A tawny owl once sat in a tree in Hyde Park for so long that birdwatchers visiting from all over the country could depend upon seeing it. Owls in particular, with their flat faces and human-seeming gaze, turning their heads to look at the world even when their bodies remain rooted to the spot, are more readily portrayed than other birds.

But the nameless artist who descended beneath the earth, through narrow, airless passages and terrifying darkness to one of the deepest of all the caves of Chauvet in France, had to carry an image of an owl in his head in order to scratch it into the wall (fig. 1, p. 15). As with the real bird itself, I have only ever seen a photograph of this prehistoric depiction, which appears to have tufted ears and a far-sighted expression, so much so that ornithologists have identified it as an eagle owl, the largest and fiercest in Europe. Created more than 30,000 years ago, it is thought to be the oldest image ever made of a bird.

Only the most intrepid caver could reach it, even then, and now the caves of Chauvet have been sealed up for preservation. Why is it hidden down there? To come across it, flashing up by the light of a flame in blackness, must have been astonishing, a religious rite or event. It surely has the character of a revelation.

The bird is a mythical messenger (think of angels) or an augury of the future (think of the the Romans and the Etruscans poring over birds' entrails) (fig. 4, p. 146). Egyptian gods have the head of a bird; bulls and dragons are winged; griffons have both wings and eagle talons. Western art depicts the Holy Spirit as a dove hovering above a sacred figure in a blaze of white light: the bird as UFO (cat. 40, pp. 132–133).

A bird is the spirit of light in itself, of energy, prospect and vitality. It tells us the time – cock crow and starling murmuration – and forecasts the weather. Swallows fly high when it is dry, low when rain is coming; seagulls wing their way inland when a storm is impending at sea. The flight of geese over Ancient Egypt announced the shifting of the seasons, just as their sorrowful departure for warmer climes heralds winter in Europe. In art they may be a warning. Those black crows flying up from the cornfield in Van Gogh's late painting, as if scattered by the crack of a gun, seem to sense the fatal future.

The beauty of birds is hardly the only reason we have to depict them. We would not have paintings of shoebills, American flamingos or even humdrum sparrows if that were true. Birds invite and require an attentiveness far beyond other creatures. You can hear them even when you cannot see them. A whole genre of Japanese painting exists to express the elusiveness of birds, full-throated yet invisible in nature, just as they are hidden within the image.

Hokusai's wondrous *Bullfinch and Weeping Cherry* shows pink and white flowers blossoming in brilliant cobalt space (fig. 5). There is no sense of gravity and at first the eponymous bird is barely visible, apparently hanging upside down. So giddy is this sense of floating among bright petals, the bird no help with optical orientation, that this woodblock print is sometimes displayed the wrong way up. Our eyes, and the bullfinch itself, are lost in nature.

A bird can amplify the figure in a portrait. Holbein's *Lady with a Squirrel and a Starling* features a long-nosed and somewhat sullen woman who might otherwise be unappealing. But her bony features are balanced by the soft squirrel, its tail gently covering her cleavage, her nose mitigated by the lively beak of the starling perched on a twig beside her. In Holbein's magnificent portrait of the hawkish Robert Cheseman, as sharp-beaked as the royal falcon on his arm, the bird is the counterpart of the man. His hand is so delicately restraining the bird it is more like a caress. Cheseman is supposed to have been falconer to Henry VIII, though this is disputed. Either way, the portrait speaks to his desire to be seen with this bird (cat. 12, p. 73).

Art may aspire to be bird-like – delicate, airborne – and yet remain earthbound. Brancusi aims for a sense of avian flight with his brass sculpture *Bird in Space*, which rises like a streamlined wing but gets its motion from the shifting radiance of its lightning-bright surface. Stunning as it is, and the very embodiment of aspiration, his bird remains tethered to its weighty plinth (cat. 37, p. 121).

Forever young, forever strange, no matter that we cage or tame them, birds may inspire works of art without ever quite – or entirely - alighting inside them. It is not just that early painters often worked with corpses or stuffed skins, with no sense of how their subjects moved or behaved in reality. Nor is it that poetry carries the dematerialising spirit of birds so well, from Shelley's joyous skylark (p. 183) to Dickinson's darting soul of hope. It is that art must keep a bird captive in order to capture its essence.

And perhaps that is why *The Goldfinch* of Carel Fabritius rises so high above other images, so to speak, in its peerless portrait of the little bird on its perch, so abrupt and austere, one eye glistening as it turns its head out of profile towards you, face to face in this sudden moment of noticing each other across time and space. Fabritius stills the goldfinch twice: once by showing it imprisoned by the chain around its leg, so that it can never fly away. And again within the frame, for it can never escape this painting. The beauty of Fabritius's masterpiece is in exact tension with its poignancy: the enigmatic bird, so gentle and solitary, with its flash of golden wing, its alert eye and yearning body, perhaps still full of hope, held here before you as a fellow being, captive, no longer on the wing. It is the greatest painting of a bird in all art.

FIG. 5
Katsushika Hokusai, *Bullfinch and Weeping Cherry (Uso, shidarezakura)*, c. 1829–1839.
Woodblock print from an untitled series of flowers and birds, 254 × 191 mm.
Clarence Buckingham Collection, The Art Institute of Chicago.

What If All the Birds Fell Out of the Sky?

Philip Hoare

FIG. 1
Roelant Savery, *Orpheus Charming the Animals with his Music*, 1627. Oil on panel, 62 × 131.5 cm. Mauritshuis, The Hague.

On a widescreen canvas as crowded as a ring road at rush hour, Roelant Savery's painting of 1627, *Orpheus Charming the Animals with his Music,* depicts a scene from Ovid's *Metamorphoses*. In it, Savery performs the same miracle as the legendary poet with his lyre, summoning birds of every kind of feather, from the skies and the trees (along with a ghostly horse and a pair of lions after slumber among the cockatoos).

It's a kind of collision, a seventeenth-century virtual reality. Like moths on a car windscreen on a night drive, they hover in a filmy layer, both there and not there at the same time. In Savery's careful hand they strike you as strangely static, like shiny Victorian scraps in an album, or those semi-transparent transfers I loved when I was a boy, with images of dinosaurs or scuba-divers that, when rubbed down with a pencil, could be magically embedded in pre-printed scenes of Jurassic jungles or underwater reefs out of my dreams.

Like the dinosaurs from whom they are indeed descended, birds have an eerie ability to appear as aliens on our planet, as if they were only here on a visit. Perhaps that's why they seem so Edenic to us: they occupy an extra dimension that we are denied; as if, like the whales who left the land for the sea and induced all that jealousy in us, so birds escaped all our earthly sins as they pursued their airy delights.

Savery's painting is idyllic. But it is also somewhat surreal, and as I look at it on my computer screen, glowing darkly with pixels per inch, I feel a strange, itchy sense of worry and uncertainty as it resolves itself. In my mind's eye, I imagine that multitudinous scene lurching into chaos, like a dread panorama by the early nineteenth-century disaster specialist John Martin or a doomsday search on AI, and it occurs to me,

What if... all the birds fell out of the sky?

...en masse, like one giant cloud, black and grey and turquoise and white, crimson and emerald and cerise. All the shearwaters no longer shearing the waves. All the birds-no-longer-of-paradise, legless because that's the way they reached Europe, sent back as skins, forever in the act of falling down. All the ravens deprived of their sooty black holes that they make in the sky. All the sunbirds faltering as if the sun had melted their waxen wings. All the eagles losing their dare, as if someone flicked a switch somewhere and subjected them to the deadening gravity to which we terrestrials are forever shackled.

I see them now, plummeting like dark flecky snow. All the flighty finches and skylarks and warblers, all the noble falcons and hawks and crows, all the aristocratic cormorants and albatrosses and gulls, all the stalwart brent geese and the oystercatchers and the godwits, all felled in one enormous blow, as though we had simply stopped believing in them and, deprived of our suspension of disbelief, they had tumbled to earth, silenced in a new silent spring.

Where would all our art and our longing be then? Where all our sunrises and our poetry? All would be as nothing without these transmigratory souls.

No image of a bird is ever accurate because no bird ever stood still for their portrait. Their fleeting physical presence, being composed of feathers and bones and flesh and fresh air, militates against such capture. As Herman Melville despaired of a whale ever fairly floating itself for its portrait, so their avian cousins defy human definition. A bird, like a whale, is unpainted to the last. Pluck an owl of its feathers and its predatory puffiness, and what would you have left? Nothing unrecognisable, to recall Melville, when he stated you could gain no real impression of a whale from their bones.

The skeleton of a bird would leave an alien clueless. Their very featheriness, their volume and their presence is a magical act, sustaining an illusion, a flickering trick of the light. Feathers, after all, are essentially air itself trapped by their barbs, the most delicate architecture borne by any animal on earth.

Aren't you jealous? We cannot relate to birds precisely because of their superpower, their mastery of the air, forever in movement, navigating thousands of migratory miles by a sheer act of will and extrasensory perception. We require vast resources to stay up there; they barely need to flick a feather to maintain their airy domain.

A gannet rises on a North Sea thermal over Bass Rock or Helgoland, then folds back those aerodynamic, superdynamic wings to slice the blue air like a blade as the bird dives, connecting its turquoise-ringed eyes to the grey ocean with prey the only thing on its mind. An avocet on the salt marshes of Hampshire or Zeeland measures out its stride like a carved ivory netsuke, wading on iridescent legs the colour of mauve enamel; then lifts into the air to become its own graphic avatar.

Eider ducks, the first animals to be protected by law by St Cuthbert on his nest-like island in the seventh century, preen their pistachio-green necks to the sun, cooing like camp comedians. In central London, pink flamingos, all looking the same, struck curious, art deco poses on the roof garden of the Biba department store as though auditioning for a film by John Waters. The brown smudge of a sparrow hops on the bike path in front of me. A swift scythes shapes out of the clouds as I glance out of my window, leaving me forlorn and wishing I possessed that graceful freedom, instead of carrying these old bones about with me all my life.

FIG. 2
Pat de Groot, *Great Cormorant*, 1991. Silkscreen from *Comorants*, portfolio of 4 prints, 965 × 483 mm. Private collection.

Unlike us, birds know what they are for and where they should be. They keep their side of the bargain. That's why we put them in cages (birds, not angels, though nothing is impossible), to contain their anarchy, reducing them to decorative objects, like Carel Fabritius's forlorn goldfinch – 'It takes a moment to notice the chain around its foot,' as Laura Cumming so plaintively declares – or Albrecht Dürer's blue roller hanging on its single nail on his studio wall, only lately lifeless, its bird-of-paradise colours already beginning to fade (fig. 3). The artist caught all the pity of the thing – all the pity of the world – in that claw tucked into its wing, in the half-open beak emitting a silent cry of pain. Nothing I could ever tell you would be as eloquent or as evocative of the gulf between us and the rest of the natural world.

William Blake saw birds as auguries of the greater extraction, in an age in which the abuse of the natural environment went hand in hand with the enslavement of people. 'A Robin Red breast in a Cage / Puts all Heaven in a Rage,' he declared in his bitingly ironic 'Auguries of Innocence'. 'A Skylark wounded in the wing, / A Cherubim does cease to sing.' 'The Game Cock clip'd & arm'd for fright / Does the Rising Sun affright.' 'The Owl that calls upon the Night / Speaks the Unbeliever's fright.' 'He who shall hurt the little Wren / Shall never be belov'd by Men.'

One of the cruellest things I ever saw – all the more cruel for its ignorance – was on a visit I made to sex-offending prisoners in a jail on an English island. They were and are the lowest of the low: the inmates of another nearby 'ordinary' prison, who made their food, would insert razor blades or broken glass into their meals. Entering the compound through a double lock (as if the convicts were to be climatically preserved as much as to be punished), I came out into the 'garden' of the prison yard. Surrounded by the men who spend 23 out of 24 hours a day locked in their cells was a cage, in the middle of the yard, twice the size of one of those cells. It contained a collection of budgerigars, yellow and green and blue. With their heads bowed, they looked as unhappy as the men, their pale colours being drained away by the bars. It was a double insult: far from being a consolation to the prisoners, the birds' fate was an echo of the men's confinement. A life sentence for them, too.

Punished for their impudence in leaving our land for their sky or sea, birds and whales suffer for our vanity and our jealousy. The grebes and egrets of the waters where I swim were, within the lifetime of my grandmother, slaughtered to provide hats for ladies of fashion, just as those feminine (and many masculine) waists were constrained by the feathery baleen plates ripped out of right whales' mouths. We cannot sustain their fearful beauty; therefore birds must die every second, everywhere.

Every year, 100,000 song birds are trapped in mist nets and caught on glue-covered sticks on Mediterranean islands for sport or consumption; 47 million game birds – was there ever such an anthropocentric name? – are bred for shooting in Scotland and other Western nations; and 10 million ducks are shot in the US, their floppy bodies retrieved by dogs we have made complicit in the slaughter.

Mark that on your weekly calendar. Two hundred million chickens culled every day for our menus. Debeaked, declawed, all these birds go undrawn, hidden by our shame. Meanwhile, their wild cousins appear as just so much aerial litter in the sky.

Every kind of bird he could gather, and many others he could not, are summoned to Savery's art by the art of Orpheus's lyre. They become super-real objects as a result. Isolated, insular, they might be hanging by monofilament from the top of the frame, dangling like model aircraft from a boy's bedroom ceiling (fig. 1). Birds arrayed for our admiration, not their utility, studding the sky and the trees like jewels in a crown.

I can find 69 birds in the painting – you may discover more – versus only 12 animals. A pair of macaws converse. Storks seem to stand in mid-air. You can see where Savery's fascination lies. These are academic birds, assembled and stuffed for the occasion. A dodo perches on a rock, posing for its role in *Alice's Adventures in Wonderland* (John Tenniel's illustration for Lewis Carroll's book directly drew on Savery's original – figs. 4 and 5).

FIG. 3
Albrecht Dürer, *Dead Blue Roller*, c. 1500. Watercolour and gouache on parchment, 274 × 198 mm. Albertina, Vienna.

FIG. 4
John Tenniel, *Dodo*, in 'A Caucus Race and a Long Tale', in Lewis Carroll, *Alice's Adventures in Wonderland*, 1865. Library of Congress, Washington, DC.

FIG. 5
Roelant Savery (attributed), *Dodo and Other Birds*, c. 1625–1630. Oil on canvas, 82 × 102 cm. Natural History Museum, London.

They all appear a little awkward, head-heavy, stiff-legged, barely built for flight. The rhino, the camel and the goat standing on the cliff in the top right look as if they might take off into the air. But you've got to hand it to the artist for his sheer chutzpah. There's something wonderfully teenage about the whole affair, all those gawky, plumed gatecrashers descending on the memory of a free festival as the sun came down.

In my imagination they are joined by their ancestors, the rainbow-feathered archaeopteryx and leathery pterosaurs and the giant moas of the land of the long white cloud. All those hesitant birds that stare at us glassy-eyed from glass cabinets and museum dioramas, from Manhattan and Berlin and Amsterdam to Hobart and South Kensington, escaping their dusty plaster and straw guts, ready to rise again, resurrected, pecking and cawing and calling and singing and soaring out of our dreams and into a brave new avian home of their own.

Here they all are! The millions of slain passenger pigeons are restored to the North American skies; the great auks, the penguins of the north, are saved from the guns on icy Arctic isles; the dodos made de-extinct in their Mauritian fastness, no longer sitting targets with those unflappable wings. Clucking and clicking and cooing, all of them are gloriously, impossibly returned to audition for a role in Savery's immersive theatre of avian display.

I hereby reassure you, here and now, that far from an augury of extinction, Savery's epic is in fact a stupendous vision of what might have been and could yet be. A feverish, fluttering work of art filled with that same impulse present in each and every one of us: the desire to be set free. After all, who among you could go outside and look at a bird in the sky and not see your own soul up there?

Carpaccio and Birds

Stefan Hertmans

FIG. 1
Vittore Carpaccio, *Young Knight in a Landscape*, c. 1510. Oil on canvas, 218.5 × 151.5 cm.
Museo Nacional Thyssen-Bornemisza, Madrid.

The first bird to fascinate me was a painted one: the white peacock in a painting by Melchior d'Hondecoeter. It dominates one of the most famous poultry yard scenes by the seventeenth-century Dutch painter. The prominently depicted bird turns its head menacingly towards several smaller birds; in the half-light of my childhood bedroom, it often frightened me – my grandfather had painted a copy of it. Perhaps that is why I have always looked at birds in paintings with such interest. In time, I came to understand that they often possess a strong symbolic meaning – each bird tells a story, lends depth to a scene, comments on it or adds a touch of irony. The animals embody moral qualities, spiritual themes or sensual motifs.

Young Knight in a Landscape by the Venetian painter Vittore Carpaccio (1465–1525) also features many birds – Carpaccio is known for frequently staging birds in striking positions and enigmatic settings. Well-known examples include the red parrot in *The Baptism of the Selenites* (once copied by a spell-bound John Ruskin); the suggestive turtle-doves in the double portrait of *Two Venetian Ladies*; and the diving cormorants helping the young men to fish in *Hunting on the Lagoon* with, in the background, geese soaring in a V formation.

In the portrait of the mysterious knight (whose identity has been the subject of much debate), the background is filled with all kinds of birds. A few songbirds dive from the branches of a scrawny little tree (the likes of which Carpaccio often painted), as does a jay with feathers standing up on its head; on the other side of the bare tree sits a small, dove-like falcon; a white heron rests down by the water while, in the background, a vulture seems to be pulling entrails from a vague shape (with some unsuspecting rabbits in the grass nearby); and in the upper-left background, a stork stands on its nest. But what really catches the attention – and has led to all kinds of speculation over the centuries – are the two birds turning around each other at the top left, which seem to be caught in a dance-like fight: a heron and a falcon. They hang high in the picture, pinned against a backdrop of white summer clouds. The falcon leans to the right into the picture, the heron faces left. The heron is on its back, facing skyward, its neck bent back as if ready to strike out in defence. The falcon occupies the dominant position above it and seems about to attack. Has anyone ever seen a heron and a falcon engage in aerial combat? It is undoubtedly a very rare occurrence, and the only falcon capable of confronting a heron would probably be the peregrine falcon. Why did Carpaccio, whose admiration for nature and animals was almost pantheistic, add this eccentric scene to the life-size portrait of a nobleman?

To find out what the birds mean, we must focus on the prominently depicted young knight and, in fact, first on the stoat in its white winter coat in the bottom left corner of the painting. It suggests that the knight depicted belonged to the Order of the Ermine, an order of knights of French origin whose founding date is uncertain. Just above the ermine, an unfolded note reveals the order's motto: *Malo mori quam foedari* (I would rather die than be dishonoured).

On the whole, it is an enchanting portrait, one of the first full-length, life-size portraits in European painting. The young man in an elegant suit of armour makes a highly refined impression. His features are somewhat feminine, and his long ginger hair hangs down to his shoulders. His gaze is almost dreamy, but his right hand rests on the pommel of his sword and his left grips the sheath, as if he were ready to draw and fight. It is merely a pose, however: the young man wants to show his knightly fighting spirit, but the idyllic surroundings with the enigmatic birds provide the portrait with such a poetic, graceful context that we cannot but see the portrayed knight as an ethereal apparition. Although he stands life-size before us, he does not look at us; his gaze is directed at something outside the frame. In the middle ground on the left, we see a young boy on horseback, wearing a helmet. Perhaps it is the knight's squire, awaiting his orders, or perhaps it is the knight himself when he was young, ready for a joust. To the right of the man's feet (from our viewpoint), white lilies are in bloom, symbolising virginal purity, but a broken tree stump nearby seems to predict an early death – an Orphic symbol that finds a visual echo on his other side. Indeed, on his left (from our viewpoint), a purple and a white iris are also in flower – perhaps symbolising his fate between peace and combat? Everything is allegory and subtlety; at the back right, a deer with large antlers near the water turns away from us as it gazes over a landscape that is not visible to us. A sign hanging on the facade to the left shows a leaping

FIG. 2
Vittore Carpaccio, *Young Knight in a Landscape*, c. 1510 (detail). Oil on canvas, 218,5 × 151,5 cm. Museo Nacional Thyssen-Bornemisza, Madrid.

horse whose hooves seem to graze a peacock's beak. If you trace sightlines from the various figures, you end up with a confusing network of possible perspectives. Subtly painted herbs are in blossom; the shadow cast by a rock resembles a bent leg; a jet of water flows from a pipe bearing a strong anatomical resemblance to male genitalia; two dogs watch from either side, the one on the left looking rather droopy, the other on the right rather snarly – this is clearly not *their* hunt.

What is actually happening here? The knight exudes a suggestive reserve: is he thinking about the dilemma between courtly love and knightly combat? If so, the two birds frozen mid-air in their dance-like fight form an allegory of his dilemma. That the falcon symbolises his fighting spirit goes without saying; but a fighting heron is something we can barely imagine. The heron is usually depicted as a waiting spectator, a motionless bird beside the water, a meditative figure often reflected in the slight ripples beneath which it suspects fish (which have always symbolised the soul). Indeed, this 'true' version of the bird is seen standing in the water at the back right, staring as if it were the philosopher among birds. But here it is on its back, its legs sticking up awkwardly in the air, a fighting pose that is rather laughable.

What do these birds tell us about the main figure, with his hand on his sword? It is as if the musing young man is about to get involved in a fight against his will and which he may not be able to win; he is of too elegant, too pensive a nature for that. The fighting falcon and the heron aptly depict this cultural dilemma during the late age of knighthood; the cultivated and refined aristocratic young men who were trained for knighthood were generally less interested in the rough fighting culture of their forefathers. This knight is indeed of noble birth – although he has been assigned many identities over the years, the most widely accepted is that he is the third Duke of Urbino. In any case, he clearly does not wish to be prey for the falcon. The courtly aspect of his appearance is further represented by other birds: in the middle ground, above a town built into a mountain, a second heron can be seen in flight, its neck bent just as strangely as the fighting heron (herons do bend their necks in flight, but not as artificially as Carpaccio would have us believe – his work often contains subtle visual irony). This visual echo has an almost comical effect, as if this second bird were mocking the absurd posture of its prominent companion, namely, the madness of a heron wanting to take on a falcon in aerial combat. This little game becomes even more cunning when we realise that it is impossible to tell whether it is a heron or a stork standing in the nest on the roof at the back left. Both bird species make rather irregular nests out of branches. Herons usually build their nests by the water's edge, close to the ground, while storks are known to prefer higher places. In flying towards the nest on the left in the background, is the heron making it clear to the knight that he should choose a love nest over fighting? Even though this knight would rather die than be dishonoured, it seems that his honour lies more in *not* having to engage in fighting. He possesses both character traits: he is both a thinker and a doer, a man who lives on beauty and reflection, and yet wants to defend himself, the product of a long courtly tradition. Carpaccio shows us this ambivalence in a poetic and suggestive way through 'the fowls of the air' and the icons from his pictorial paradise. Thus, the dancing-fighting heron and falcon depict both the inward struggle and the cultural ambivalence of the courtly knight. It is a snapshot of a turning point in European history, a particular moment in which the knight's complex, even erotic, identity is portrayed in a nature scene in which nothing is natural anymore and everything stands for something else. They seem to be intellectual *concetti* of a rapidly vanishing world, captured for us in its enchanting fleetingness, gliding figures of a spiritual, fascinating richness.

Birds

in World Literature

Introduction by Simon Schama

The complicated, insistent, fateful relationship between the human and avian worlds has been registered not just in images but also in literature. So it seemed right to acknowledge that with an anthology, in both poetry and prose, drawn from cultures as distant from each other in time and place as the Latin verse of Catullus; the Tang-dynasty Chinese poetry of Bai Juyi; medieval English fable; Edgar Allen Poe's unwelcome herald of doom, the raven; twentieth-century Suriname; and Italo Calvino's analytically beautiful description of a starling murmuration over Rome (where I too witnessed that astounding spectacle). Inevitably, the choices made by Martine Gosselink and I reflect our personal tastes and enthusiasms, but we have tried our best to encompass what, quite often literally, is meant by 'points of view': thirteen of them in the case of Wallace Stevens's blackbird, but just the one predator inhabited by Ted Hughes's *Hawk Roosting*, while the thirteenth-century Persian poet Rūmī addresses a falcon directly, as does Shelley's metaphysical rapture to the skylark ('Bird thou never wert').

Some of the most intense and powerful responses to the world of birds have been registered in charged, high-voltage prose. Daphne du Maurier's *The Birds* is one of the most terrifying stories of world literature, concentrating in its merciless power the fears that have fluttered through human imagination. Even more sinister than the film Alfred Hitchcock made of it, its steel-cut writing takes off in some places, wheeling malevolently over the doomed hiding places of its victims. And no anthology could possibly be complete without Rachel Carson's cautionary fable of a *Silent Spring;* prefacing her impassioned polemic against the feckless use of pesticides, this is the book that, arguably, launched the modern environmental movement.

But the literary buffet we have cooked up for you is meant less as moral nourishment (though that need not be excluded) than an invitation to feast on great writing about the inexhaustible subject of *The Goldfinch*'s winged friends and ours.

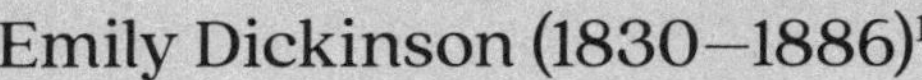

Emily Dickinson (1830–1886)[1]

I hope you love birds too. It is economical. It saves going to heaven.

FROM

Thunderclap: A Memoir of Art and Life and Sudden Death
Laura Cumming (b. 1961)[2]

The first sight of The Goldfinch *is abrupt and austere. The little bird appears on its perch, so quick and alert, dark against the wall that receives its hovering shadow. One eye glistens as it turns its head out of profile towards you. You must not disturb the millisecond in which this winged creature looks straight at you, eye to eye, and yet of course it can never fly away. It takes a moment to notice the chain around its leg. So delicate as to be almost imperceptible, this chain is viciously cruel, tethering the bird to the spot. The beauty of the painting is in equal tension with its almost unbearable poignancy: the captive bird so enigmatic, a mortal being made apparent to us for all time yet forever imprisoned by the chain (and the picture frame). There is not another painting like it.*

Fabritius's goldfinch is an adult male with a soft reddish-brown head, a glittering eye and a lightning flash of yellow on its wing. It has gone as far as it can towards the edge of the ledge, and the picture. There it turns back to look at you in a frisson of noticing, and being noticed. This is no generalised bird of the sort in those days kept for pets, and then depicted in supposedly amusing paintings in which they perform the trick of drawing water from their own little well with a tiny cup on a chain. This bird has a specific force of personality, an air of solitude and sorrow, a living being looking out at another living being from its prison against the wall. This painting is a portrait....

Anyone who has ever seen goldfinches fluttering and chattering and alighting on seedheads in meadows, or watched them bumbling through the thistledown they love, will know why the word charm was chosen for their collective noun. A charm of goldfinches soars at dusk, swoops at dawn, sings upliftingly in summer trees. In flight, the yellow stripe spreads into a golden cape.... In the gallery, where the bird's shadow flitters against the white wall, the yellow stripe glows at a distance. It is painted with a long-lost colour called lead-tin-yellow, made using an oxide that produced an opaque and saturated brilliance. But lead-tin-yellow, so often used in Delft for the peel of a lemon or a woman's velvet jacket, was potentially poisonous if ingested. Nobody makes it now. It has disappeared from art and memory....

...The Goldfinch *is not a trick. The picture departs entirely from the optical illusion that is conventionally cited as its great achievement. With trompe l'oeil, you should not be able to see in the same instant that you come across it that the goldfinch is quite clearly made of paint. Yet this is what his masterpiece immediately and openly declares. This bird is conspicuously created out of pigment and brushstrokes and you can even count them: one for each feather on the wings, one for the patch by the beak, the amazing flash of yellow through which Fabritius has scored the end of his brush.*

These strokes are all visible, not too much strenuous colour, not too much ornithological detail: as gentle as the bird itself. The wall is a feat of shadow play; the bars of the perch, the bird's claws, the individual links of the gold chain are all painted in the finest threads of light pigment.... It is both a magnificent feat of persuasive depiction and at the same time its exact opposite; the signature conspicuously lettered on the flat surface. Fabritius sets up an illusion and undermines it all at once: the goldfinch to the life, but as a spirit of paint.

'A Little Bird'
Alexander Pushkin (1799–1837)[3]

In alien lands devoutly clinging
To age-old rites of Russian earth,
I let a captive bird go winging
To greet the radiant spring's rebirth.
My heart grew lighter then: why mutter
Against God's providence, and rage,
When I was free to set aflutter
But one poor captive from his cage!

'Sparrows in Winter'
Yang Wan-li (1127–1206)[4]

hundreds of sparrows
crowd the empty courtyard in winter
they puff in their feathers
high on the plum branches
they are saying what a fine evening this is
what a noise they make to disturb me
suddenly they disappear in a startled flock
and the world is as still as death

FROM

H is for Hawk
Helen Macdonald (b. 1970)[5]

The hawk had filled the house with wildness as a bowl of lilies fills a house with scent.

'Hawk Roosting'
Ted Hughes (1930–1998)[6]

I sit in the top of the wood, my eyes closed.
Inaction, no falsifying dream
Between my hooked head and hooked feet:
Or in sleep rehearse perfect kills and eat.

The convenience of the high trees!
The air's buoyancy and the sun's ray
Are of advantage to me;
And the earth's face upward for my inspection.

My feet are locked upon the rough bark.
It took the whole of Creation
To produce my foot, my each feather:
Now I hold Creation in my foot

Or fly up, and revolve it all slowly –
I kill where I please because it is all mine.
There is no sophistry in my body:
My manners are tearing off heads –

The allotment of death.
For the one path of my flight is direct
Through the bones of the living.
No arguments assert my right:

The sun is behind me.
Nothing has changed since I began.
My eye has permitted no change.
I am going to keep things like this.

Franz Kafka (1883–1924)[7]

I am a cage, in search of a bird.

'How Did You Get Away'
Rūmī (1207–1273)[8]

How did you get away?
You were the pet falcon of an old woman.
Did you hear the falcon-drum?
You were a drunken songbird put in with owls.
Did you smell the odour of a garden?
You got tired of sour fermenting
and left the tavern.

You went like an arrow to the target
from the bow of time and place.
The man who stays at the cemetery pointed the way,
but you didn't go.
You became light and gave up wanting to be famous.
You don't worry about what you're going to eat,
so why buy an engraved belt?

I've heard of living at the centre, but what about
leaving the centre of the centre?
Flying toward thankfulness, you become
the rare bird with one wing made of fear,
and one of hope. In autumn,
a rose crawling along the ground in the cold wind.
Rain on the roof runs down and out by the spout
as fast as it can.

Talking is pain. Lie down and rest,
now that you've found a friend to be with.

'Feeling Like a Crane'
Bai Juyi (772–846)[9]

Well, here's a crane without a flock –
Flying, always flying, to rest in wild fields.
To keep from starving, he pecks at decaying mice.
To stave off thirst, he steals a drink where he can.

Chaste and handsome, by nature upright and honest,
Compared to other birds, how graceful he is.
Like them, he wanders, but with different aspirations.
And he's been this way ten years or more.

He rises, addicted to the desire
To pull against the hand that holds him back.
His proud swagger fills the small ponds he lights in,
As he tries to eat before the local chickens get it all.

He yearns for paddies ripe with rice
As he struggles with the smell of rotten fish.
He yearns to find his right master
As he struggles with the crowd of crows and kites.

No one can really know his wild heart.
His nature is, well, changeable.
Even when he's well-fed, he'd rather remain like this
Than perch up high on some Imperial pavilion.

FROM

The Owl and the Nightingale
Anonymous, England (12th–13th c.)[10]

The owl waited until it was evening; she couldn't hold back any longer, because she was so angry that she could hardly breathe, and finally she spoke: 'How does my song seem to you now? Do you think that I can't sing just because I can't twitter? You often insult me and say things to upset and embarrass me. If I held you in my talons if only I could! and you were off your branch, you'd sing a very different tune!'

The nightingale answered, 'As long as I keep out of the open, and protect myself against being exposed, I'm not bothered about your threats; as long as I stay put in my hedge, I don't care at all what you say. I know that you're ruthless towards those who can't protect themselves from you, and that where you can you bully small birds cruelly and harshly. That is why all kinds of birds hate you, and they all drive you away, and screech and scream around you, and mob you at close quarters; and for the same reason even the titmouse would gladly rip you to pieces.

'You're ugly to look at, and hideous in all sorts of ways; your body is squat, your neck is scrawny, your head is bigger than the rest of you put together; your eyes are black as coal, and as big as if they were painted with woad. You glare as if you want to bite to death everything that you can strike with your talons. Your beak is hard and sharp, and curved like a bent hook. You often make a repeated clacking noise with it, and that's one of your songs. But you're making threats against my person, and would like to crush me with your talons; a frog would suit you better, squatting under a mill-wheel; snails, mice, and other vermin would be more natural and appropriate for you. You roost by day and fly by night; you show that you're an evil creature.

'You are loathsome and unclean I'm talking about your nest, and also about your dirty chicks; you're bringing them up with really filthy habits. You know very well what they do in their nest: they foul it up to the chin; they sit there as if they're blind. There's a proverb about that: "Shame on the creature which fouls its own nest"!

'The other year a falcon was breeding; she didn't guard her nest well. You crept in there one day, and laid your filthy egg in it. When the time came that she hatched the eggs and the chicks emerged, she

brought her chicks food, watched over the nest and saw them eat; she saw that on one side her nest was fouled on the outer edge. The falcon was angry with her chicks, and screamed loudly, and scolded sternly: "Tell me, who's done this? It was never your nature to do this kind of thing. This is a disgusting thing to have happened to you. Tell me, if you know who did it!"

'Then they all said, "It was actually our brother, the one over there with the big head – it's a pity nobody's cut it off! Throw him out as a reject, so that he breaks his neck!" The Falcon believed her chicks, and seized that dirty chick by the middle, and threw it off that wild branch, where magpies and crows tore it to pieces.

'There's a fable told about this, though it's not entirely a fable: this is what happens to the villain who's come from a disreputable family and mixes with respectable people; he's always letting his origins show, that he's come from a rotten egg even if he's turned up in a respectable nest; even if an apple rolls away from the tree where it was growing with the others, although it's some distance from it it still reflects clearly where it's come from.'

The nightingale replied with these words, and after that long speech she sang as loudly and as shrilly as if a resonant harp were being played.

The owl listened to this, and kept her eyes lowered, and sat puffed up and swollen with rage, as if she had swallowed a frog, because she was fully aware that the nightingale was singing to humiliate her.

'The Raven and the Fox'
Jean de La Fontaine (1621–1695)[11]

Master Raven, perched upon a tree,
Held in his beak a savoury piece of cheese;
Its pleasant odour, borne upon the breeze,
Allured Sir Reynard, with his flattery.
'Ha! Master Raven, 'morrow to you, sir;
How black and glossy! now, upon my word,
I never – beautiful! I do aver.
If but your voice becomes your coat, no bird
More fit to be the Phœnix of our wood –
I hope, sir, I am understood?'
The Raven, flattered by the praise,
Opened his spacious beak, to show his ways
Of singing: down the good cheese fell.
Quick the Fox snapped it. 'My dear sir, 'tis well,'
He said. 'Know that a flatterer lives
On him to whom his praise he gives;
And, my dear neighbour, an' you please,
This lesson's worth a slice of cheese.' –
The Raven, vexed at his consenting,
Flew off, too late in his repenting.

'The Tame Bird Was in a Cage'
Rabindranath Tagore (1861–1941)[12]

The tame bird was in a cage,
the free bird was in the forest.
They met when the time came,
it was a decree of fate.
The free bird cries, 'O my love,
let us fly to the wood.'
The cage bird whispers,
'Come hither, let us both live in the cage.'
Says the free bird, 'Among bars,
where is there room to spread one's wings?'
'Alas,' cries the caged bird, 'I should
not know where to sit perched in the sky.'

The free bird cries, 'My darling,
sing the songs of the woodlands.'
The cage bird sings, 'Sit by my side,
I'll teach you the speech of the learned.'
The forest bird cries, 'No, ah no!
songs can never be taught.'
The cage bird says, 'Alas for me,
I know not the songs of the woodlands.'

Their love is intense with longing,
but they never can fly wing to wing.
Through the bars of the cage they look,
and vain is their wish to know each other.
They flutter their wings in yearning, and sing,
'Come closer, my love!'
The free bird cries, 'It cannot be,
I fear the closed doors of the cage.'
The cage bird whispers,
'Alas, my wings are powerless and dead.'

FROM

Fragments Out of the Deluge VIII: But the Sunbird

Christopher Okigbo (1932–1967)[13]

BUT the Sunbird –
Listen under the oilbean shadows –
Repeats, repeats,
over the oilbean shadows...

A fleet of eagles
over the oilbean shadows
Holds the square
under curse of their rank breath.

Beaks of bronze, wings of
hard-tanned felt,
The eagles flow
over man mountains,
Steep walls of voices,
horizons;
The eagles furrow
dazzling over the voices
With wings like
combs in the wind's hair.

Out of the solitude,
The fleet,
out of the solitude,
Intangible
like the silk thread of the sunlight,
The eagles ride low,
resplendent... resplendent...

And small birds sing in shadows,
Wobbling under their bones.

So squatting,
A blind dog howls at his godmother –

YUNICE at the passageway,
Singing the moon to sleep over the hills,
YUNICE at the passageway –

Give him no chair, they say,
The crier of the dawn,
Riding with gods and the angry stars
Toward the great sunshine.

'An Exuberant Song or What?'

Michaël Slory (1935–2018)[14]

On top of the roofs
of the houses

Great kiskadees up there
you swing
on the roofs
of the houses
shouting, calling,
seeking attention.
But the boys wind
one after the other
on their bicycles
on their way to a football field.

So also the cars,
zooming
past them
on the road
to take a turn
or go straight ahead.

It bothers me
even though I calmly walk on:
Look how smoothly everything is going.
Why do you worry
about all the fuss and palaver?
Worry about yourself.
After all, people
have nothing to do with you.

That's not what the jubilant song
from so high above on the house is about,
as far as you can listen to it,
as far as you can enjoy the sound?

FROM

'Three Little Birds'
Bob Marley (1945–1981)[15]

Rise up this morning,
Smiled with the rising sun,
Three little birds,
Pitch by my doorstep,
Singing sweet songs

Don't worry about a thing
Cause every little thing gonna be alright

'To a Skylark'
Percy Bysshe Shelley (1792–1822)[16]

Hail to thee, blithe Spirit!
Bird thou never wert,
That from Heaven, or near it,
Pourest thy full heart
In profuse strains of unpremeditated art.

Higher still and higher
From the earth thou springest
Like a cloud of fire;
The blue deep thou wingest,
And singing still dost soar,
and soaring ever singest.

In the golden lightning
Of the sunken sun,
O'er which clouds are bright'ning,
Thou dost float and run;
Like an unbodied joy
whose race is just begun.

The pale purple even
Melts around thy flight;
Like a star of Heaven,
In the broad day-light
Thou art unseen,
but yet I hear thy shrill delight,

Keen as are the arrows
Of that silver sphere,
Whose intense lamp narrows
In the white dawn clear
Until we hardly see, we feel that it is there.

All the earth and air
With thy voice is loud,
As, when night is bare,
From one lonely cloud
The moon rains out her beams,
and Heaven is overflow'd.

What thou art we know not;
What is most like thee?
From rainbow clouds there flow not
Drops so bright to see
As from thy presence showers
a rain of melody.

Like a Poet hidden
In the light of thought,
Singing hymns unbidden,
Till the world is wrought
To sympathy with hopes and fears
it heeded not:

Like a high-born maiden
In a palace-tower,
Soothing her love-laden
Soul in secret hour
With music sweet as love,
which overflows her bower:

Like a glow-worm golden
In a dell of dew,
Scattering unbeholden
Its aëreal hue
Among the flowers and grass,
which screen it from the view:

Like a rose embower'd
In its own green leaves,
By warm winds deflower'd,
Till the scent it gives
Makes faint with too much sweet those
heavy-winged thieves:

Sound of vernal showers
On the twinkling grass,
Rain-awaken'd flowers,
All that ever was
Joyous, and clear, and fresh,
thy music doth surpass.

Teach us, Sprite or Bird,
What sweet thoughts are thine:
I have never heard
Praise of love or wine
That panted forth a flood of
rapture so divine.

Chorus Hymeneal,
Or triumphal chant,
Match'd with thine would be all
But an empty vaunt,
A thing wherein we feel there
is some hidden want.

What objects are the fountains
Of thy happy strain?
What fields, or waves, or mountains?
What shapes of sky or plain?
What love of thine own kind?
what ignorance of pain?

With thy clear keen joyance
Languor cannot be:
Shadow of annoyance
Never came near thee:
Thou lovest: but ne'er
knew love's sad satiety.

Waking or asleep,
Thou of death must deem
Things more true and deep
Than we mortals dream,
Or how could thy notes flow in
such a crystal stream?

We look before and after,
And pine for what is not:
Our sincerest laughter
With some pain is fraught;
Our sweetest songs are those that tell
of saddest thought.

Yet if we could scorn
Hate, and pride, and fear;
If we were things born
Not to shed a tear,
I know not how thy joy we ever
should come near.

Better than all measures
Of delightful sound,
Better than all treasures
That in books are found,
Thy skill to poet were,
thou scorner of the ground!

Teach me half the gladness
That thy brain must know,
Such harmonious madness
From my lips would flow
The world should listen then,
as I am listening now.

'Split the Lark'
Emily Dickinson (1830–1886)[17]

Split the Lark
and you'll find the Music
Bulb after Bulb, in Silver rolled
Scantilly dealt to the Summer Morning
Saved for your Ear when Lutes be old.

Loose the Flood
you shall find it patent –
Gush after Gush, reserved for you –
Scarlet Experiment! Sceptic Thomas!
Now, do you doubt that your Bird was true?

'I think (I have never known anyone like you)'
Al-Abbas ibn al-Ahnaf (750–809)[18]

I think (I have never known anyone like you)
that the hearts of women on earth are made of stone.
Let me sleep if I do not receive a visit from you
(perhaps a dream image will visit me when I sleep).
I cried to a flock of sandgrouse that passed by,
and said (and I have reason to cry):
Can you, flock of sandgrouse, lend me wings
so that I can fly to the one I love?
If not, who will convey my greetings?
Then I will thank him (lovers are grateful).
What sandgrouse would not help a lover?
(May it live in misery, with a broken wing!)

Oscar Wilde (1854–1900)[19]

Nature: a place where birds
fly around uncooked.

'I Once Asked a Bird'
Hāfez (1310–1390)[20]

I once asked a bird,
how is it that you fly
in this gravity of darkness?
The bird responded, 'Love lifts me.'

'Blackbird'
Paul McCartney (b. 1942) and John Lennon (1940–1980)[21]

Blackbird singing in the dead of night
Take these broken wings and learn to fly
All your life
You were only waiting for this moment to arise

Blackbird singing in the dead of night
Take these sunken eyes and learn to see
All your life
You were only waiting for this moment to be free

Blackbird, fly, blackbird, fly
Into the light of a dark black night

Blackbird, fly, blackbird, fly
Into the light of a dark black night

Blackbird singing in the dead of night
Take these broken wings and learn to fly
All your life
You were only waiting for this moment to arise
You were only waiting for this moment to arise
You were only waiting for this moment to arise

'Thirteen Ways of Looking at a Blackbird'
Wallace Stevens (1879–1955)[22]

I
Among twenty snowy mountains,
The only moving thing
Was the eye of the blackbird.

II
I was of three minds,
Like a tree
In which there are three blackbirds.

III
The blackbird whirled in the autumn winds.
It was a small part of the pantomime.

IV
A man and a woman
Are one.
A man and a woman and a blackbird
Are one.

V
I do not know which to prefer,
The beauty of inflections
Or the beauty of innuendoes,
The blackbird whistling
Or just after.

VI
Icicles filled the long window
With barbaric glass.
The shadow of the blackbird
Crossed it, to and fro.
The mood
Traced in the shadow
An indecipherable cause.

VII
O thin men of Haddam,
Why do you imagine golden birds?
Do you not see how the blackbird
Walks around the feet
Of the women about you?

VIII
I know noble accents
And lucid, inescapable rhythms;
But I know, too,
That the blackbird is involved
In what I know.

IX
When the blackbird flew out of sight,
It marked the edge
Of one of many circles.

X
At the sight of blackbirds
Flying in a green light,
Even the bawds of euphony
Would cry out sharply.

XI
He rode over Connecticut
In a glass coach.
Once, a fear pierced him,
In that he mistook
The shadow of his equipage
For blackbirds.

XII
The river is moving.
The blackbird must be flying.

XIII
It was evening all afternoon.
It was snowing
And it was going to snow.
The blackbird sat
In the cedar-limbs.

FROM

Ulysses
James Joyce (1882–1941)[23]

It soared, a bird, it held its flight, a swift pure cry, soar silver orb it leaped serene, speeding, sustained, to come, don't spin it out too long long breath he breath long life, soaring high, high resplendent, aflame, crowned, high in the effulgence symbolistic, high, of the ethereal bosom, high, of the high vast irradiation everywhere all soaring all around about the all, the endlessnessnessness...

A Story of the Warlords
Oda Nobunaga (1534–1582), Toyotomi Hideyoshi (1537–1598), and Tokugawa Ieyasu (1543–1616)[24]

Oda Nobunaga:
if the cuckoo does not sing, kill it

Toyotomi Hideyoshi:
if the cuckoo does not sing, coax it

Tokugawa Ieyasu:
if the cuckoo doesn't sing, wait until it does

'Brancusi's Golden Bird'
Mina Loy (1882–1966)[25]

The toy
become the aesthetic archetype

As if
some patient peasant God
had rubbed and rubbed
the Alpha and Omega
of Form
into a lump of metal

A naked orientation
unwinged unplumed
the ultimate rhythm
has lopped the extremities
of crest and claw
from the nucleus of flight

The absolute act
of art
conformed
to continent sculpture

bare as the brow of Osiris –
this breast of revelation

an incandescent curve
licked by chromatic flames
in labyrinths of reflections

This gong
of polished hyperaesthesia
shrills with brass
as the aggressive light
strikes
its significance
The immaculate
conception
of the inaudible bird
occurs
in gorgeous reticence

FROM

Epic of Gilgamesh
Anonymous, Mesopotamia (21st –10th c. BCE)[26]

For six days and six nights the winds blew, torrent and tempest and flood overwhelmed the world, tempest and flood raged together like warring hosts. When the seventh day dawned the storm from the south subsided, the sea grew calm, the flood was stilled; I looked at the face of the world and there was silence, all mankind was turned to clay. The surface of the sea stretched as flat as a roof-top; I opened a hatch and the light fell on my face. Then I bowed low, I sat down and I wept, the tears streamed down my face, for on every side was the waste of water. I looked for land in vain, but fourteen leagues distant there appeared a mountain, and there the boat grounded; on the mountain of Nisir the boat held fast, she held fast and did not budge. One day she held, and a second day on the mountain of Nisir she held fast and did not budge. A third day, and a fourth day she held fast on the mountain and did not budge; a fifth day and a sixth day she held fast on the mountain. When the seventh day dawned I loosed a dove and let her go. She flew away, but finding no resting-place she returned. Then I loosed a swallow, and she flew away but finding no resting-place she returned. I loosed a raven, she saw that the waters had retreated, she ate, she flew around, she cawed, and she did not come back.

Genesis 8: 6–13; 19–20[27]

4 *And the ark rested in the seventh month, on the seventeenth day of the month, upon the mountains of Ararat.*

5 *And the waters decreased continually until the tenth month: in the tenth month, on the first day of the month, were the tops of the mountains seen.*

6 *And it came to pass at the end of forty days, that Noah opened the window of the ark which he had made:*

7 *And he sent forth a raven, which went forth to and fro, until the waters were dried up from off the earth.*

8 *Also he sent forth a dove from him, to see if the waters were abated from off the face of the ground;*

9 *But the dove found no rest for the sole of her foot, and she returned unto him into the ark, for the waters were on the face of the whole earth: then he put forth his hand, and took her, and pulled her in unto him into the ark.*

10 *And he stayed yet other seven days; and again he sent forth the dove out of the ark;*

11 *And the dove came in to him in the evening; and, lo, in her mouth was an olive leaf pluckt off: so Noah knew that the waters were abated from off the earth.*

12 *And he stayed yet other seven days; and sent forth the dove; which returned not again unto him any more.*

13 *And it came to pass in the six hundredth and first year, in the first month, the first day of the month, the waters were dried up from off the earth: and Noah removed the covering of the ark, and looked, and, behold, the face of the ground was dry.*

...

19 *Every beast, every creeping thing, and every fowl, and whatsoever creepeth upon the earth, after their kinds, went forth out of the ark.*

20 *And Noah builded an altar unto the LORD; and took of every clean beast, and of every clean fowl, and offered burnt offerings on the altar.*

FROM

'The Story of Sindbad the Sailor', The Arabian Nights Entertainments
Anonymous (around 8th–15th c.)[28]

By this time the sun was about to set, and all of a sudden the sky became as dark as if it had been covered with a thick cloud. I was much astonished at this sudden darkness, but much more when I found it was occasioned by a bird of a monstrous size, that came flying toward me. I remembered that I had often heard mariners speak of a miraculous bird called the roc, and conceived that the great dome which I so much admired must be its egg. In short, the bird alighted, and sat over the egg. As I perceived her coming, I crept close to the egg, so that I had before me one of the legs of the bird, which was as big as the trunk of a tree. I tied myself strongly to it with my turban, in hopes that the roc next morning would carry me with her out of this desert island. After having passed the night in this condition, the bird flew away as soon as it was daylight, and carried me so high that I could not discern the earth; she afterward descended with so much rapidity that I lost my senses. But when I found myself on the ground, I speedily untied the knot, and had scarcely done so, when the roc, having taken up a serpent of a monstrous length in her bill, flew away.

Firoez Masjriqi (9th c.–896)[29]

The arrow is a bird. Strange! Have you ever seen
A bird that hunts only souls?

FROM

'The Raven'
Edgar Allen Poe (1809–1849)[30]

Back into the chamber turning,
all my soul within me burning,
Soon again I heard a tapping somewhat
louder than before.
'Surely,' said I, 'surely that is something
at my window lattice;
Let me see, then, what thereat is,
and this mystery explore –
Let my heart be still a moment
and this mystery explore; –
'Tis the wind and nothing more!'

Open here I flung the shutter, when,
with many a flirt and flutter,
In there stepped a stately Raven
of the saintly days of yore;
Not the least obeisance made he;
not a minute stopped or stayed he;
But, with mien of lord or lady, perched
above my chamber door –
Perched upon a bust of Pallas
just above my chamber door –
Perched, and sat, and nothing more.

Then this ebony bird beguiling my sad
fancy into smiling,
By the grave and stern decorum
of the countenance it wore,
'Though thy crest be shorn and shaven,
thou,' I said, 'art sure no craven,
Ghastly grim and ancient Raven
wandering from the Nightly shore –
Tell me what thy lordly name is on
the Night's Plutonian shore!'
Quoth the Raven 'Nevermore.'

Much I marvelled this ungainly fowl
to hear discourse so plainly,
Though its answer little meaning –
little relevancy bore;
For we cannot help agreeing that
no living human being
Ever yet was blessed with seeing
bird above his chamber door –
Bird or beast upon the sculptured bust
above his chamber door,
With such name as 'Nevermore.'

But the Raven, sitting lonely on
the placid bust, spoke only
That one word, as if his soul in that
one word he did outpour.
Nothing farther then he uttered –
not a feather then he fluttered –
Till I scarcely more than muttered
'Other friends have flown before –
On the morrow he will leave me, as
my Hopes have flown before.'
Then the bird said 'Nevermore.'

'Carmen 2'
Catullus (c. 84–54 BCE)[31]

Sparrow, favourite of my girl,
with whom she is accustomed to play, whom she is accustomed to hold in her lap,
for whom, seeking greedily, she is accustomed to give her index finger
and to provoke sharp bites.
When it is pleasing for my shining desire
to make some kind of joke
and a relief of her grief.
I believe, so that her heavy passion may become quiet.
If only I were able to play with you yourself, and
to lighten the sad cares of your mind.

'Every Bird Sings According to Its Beak'
Jacob Cats (1577–1660)[32]

T'is is an old saying and a true,
That ev'ry bird sings its own note;
Nor can it any other do
But as permits its beak and throat.
Whene'er you rove thro' field or wood,
And well attend with ears and eyes,
You'll find the proverb just and good,
Whate'er the bird in shape or size.
Those which a hook'd sharp beak have got,
Are for the most part birds of prey,
And bent alone on war, they wot
No note of song or minstrelsy.
Whene'er near rivers, lake or flood
You chance a flat-beak'd bird to meet,
From groping in the slush and mud,
Be sure his voice is never sweet.
The birds with longer flute-like beak,
Might more be thought to song inclin'd,
But in their thrumming note and shriek,
No turn for melody you'll find.
I therefore say,
as far as size
And shape of beak,
nor fear protest,
That of all birds beneath the skies,
The little beaks they sing the best.
E'en thus among mankind, we see,
God gives the little now and then,
A talent rare and quality
Which he gives not to bigger men.
Of little beaks, what bird like he
Which night-thro' sings in wood and dale?
That feather'd soul of harmony,
That little beak, the nightingale!
And would you seek a tuneful throat,
You'll find throughout the feather'd throng,
The greater beak the harsher note,
The smaller beak the sweeter song.
As with the fowls of earth and air,
Not so with man
he hath no beak,
But in his mouth beyond compare
The nobler godlike power to speak!
And when he speaks in spirit kind,
What note of bird more softly sweet
To breathe the music of the mind,
When kindred hearts and spirits meet!
But when the mouth of man outpours
The blast of passion's wrathful breath,
The lion not more fiercely roars
His angry note of blood and death!
Hence what befalls mankind between,
Comes from a deeper source express'd,
Where fits, by ev'ry eye unseen
But God's, the impulse of the breast.
The mouth commands, implores, decries,
As moves the heart, and gives thereto
The tone which most its will implies,
By force or softness to subdue.
Hence ye who speak in bitter tone,
And fiercely wound another's heart,
Beware, and learn to curb thine own,
Lest it repay thee smart for smart.
As 'by his ears the ass is known',
A truth which no one can impeach,
'The man', as proverbs long have shown,
'Is known as truly by his speech'.

Rachid ibn Ishaq (9th c.)[33]

He sleeps in the hand of a girl. Sometimes
he moves a little, without the hand feeling it,
like a two-day-old bird that raises its head
towards its parents, and then,
exhausted, lets it
hang down.

A joke from the 1980s

What's the difference between sexy and kinky?
Sexy: a feather. Kinky: the whole chicken.

John Ruskin (1819–1900)[34]

I do not believe that any peacock envies another peacock his tail, because every peacock is persuaded that his own tail is the finest in the world. The consequence of this is that peacocks are peaceable birds.

FROM

'Daedalus and Icarus', Metamorphoses
Ovid (43 BCE–17/18)[35]

At the same time as he laid down the rules of flight, he fitted the newly created wings on the boy's shoulders. While he worked and issued his warnings the ageing man's cheeks were wet with tears: the father's hands trembled.

He gave a never to be repeated kiss to his son, and lifting upwards on his wings, flew ahead, anxious for his companion, like a bird, leading her fledglings out of a nest above, into the empty air. He urged the boy to follow, and showed him the dangerous art of flying, moving his own wings, and then looking back at his son.

Some angler catching fish with a quivering rod, or a shepherd leaning on his crook, or a ploughman resting on the handles of his plough, saw them, perhaps, and stood there amazed, believing them to be gods able to travel the sky.

And now Samos, sacred to Juno, lay ahead to the left (Delos and Paros were behind them), Lebinthos, and Calymne, rich in honey, to the right, when the boy began to delight in his daring flight, and abandoning his guide, drawn by desire for the heavens, soared higher. His nearness to the devouring sun softened the fragrant wax that held the wings: and the wax melted: he flailed with bare arms, but losing his oar-like wings, could not ride the air. Even as his mouth was crying his father's name, it vanished into the dark blue sea, the Icarian Sea, called after him.

The unhappy father, now no longer a father, shouted 'Icarus, Icarus where are you? Which way should I be looking, to see you?' 'Icarus' he called again. Then he caught sight of the feathers on the waves, and cursed his inventions. He laid the body to rest, in a tomb, and the island was named Icaria after his buried child.

FROM

Peter Pan
JM Barrie (1860–1937)[36]

'It's all right,' John announced, emerging from his hiding-place. 'I say, Peter, can you really fly?'
Instead of troubling to answer him Peter flew around the room, taking the mantelpiece on the way.
'How topping!' said John and Michael.
'How sweet!' cried Wendy.
'Yes, I'm sweet, oh, I am sweet!' said Peter, forgetting his manners again.
It looked delightfully easy, and they tried it first from the floor and then from the beds, but they always went down instead of up.
'I say, how do you do it?' asked John, rubbing his knee. He was quite a practical boy.
'You just think lovely wonderful thoughts,' Peter explained, 'and they lift you up in the air.'
He showed them again.
'You're so nippy at it,' John said, 'couldn't you do it very slowly once?'
Peter did it both slowly and quickly. 'I've got it now, Wendy!' cried John, but soon he found he had not. Not one of them could fly an inch, though even Michael was in words of two syllables, and Peter did not know A from Z.
Of course Peter had been trifling with them, for no one can fly unless the fairy dust has been blown on him. Fortunately, as we have mentioned, one of his hands was messy with it, and he blew some on each of them, with the most superb results.
'Now just wiggle your shoulders this way,' he said, 'and let go.'
They were all on their beds, and gallant Michael let go first. He did not quite mean to let go, but he did it, and immediately he was borne across the room.

'I flewed!' he screamed while still in mid-air.
John let go and met Wendy near the bathroom.
'Oh, lovely!'
'Oh, ripping!'
'Look at me!'
'Look at me!'
'Look at me!'
They were not nearly so elegant as Peter, they could not help kicking a little, but their heads were bobbing against the ceiling, and there is almost nothing so delicious as that. Peter gave Wendy a hand at first, but had to desist, Tink was so indignant.
Up and down they went, and round and round. Heavenly was Wendy's word.
'I say,' cried John, 'why shouldn't we all go out?'
Of course it was to this that Peter had been luring them. Michael was ready: he wanted to see how long it took him to do a billion miles. But Wendy hesitated.
'Mermaids!' said Peter again.
'Oo!'
'And there are pirates.'
'Pirates,' cried John, seizing his Sunday hat, 'let us go at once.'
It was just at this moment that Mr. and Mrs. Darling hurried with Nana out of 27. They ran into the middle of the street to look up at the nursery window; and, yes, it was still shut, but the room was ablaze with light, and most heart-gripping sight of all, they could see in shadow on the curtain three little figures in night attire circling round and round, not on the floor but in the air.
Not three figures, four!
In a tremble they opened the street door. Mr. Darling would have rushed upstairs, but Mrs. Darling signed him to go softly. She even tried to make her heart go softly. Will they reach the nursery in time? If so, how delightful for them, and we shall all breathe a sigh of relief, but there will be no story. On the other hand, if they are not in time, I solemnly promise that it will all come right in the end.
They would have reached the nursery in time had it not been that the little stars were watching them. Once again the stars blew the window open, and that smallest star of all called out:
'Cave, Peter!'
Then Peter knew that there was not a moment to lose. 'Come,' he cried imperiously, and soared out at once into the night, followed by John and Michael and Wendy.
Mr. and Mrs. Darling and Nana rushed into the nursery too late. The birds were flown.

FROM

Mr Palomar

Italo Calvino (1923–1985)[37]

If he lingers for a few moments to observe the arrangement of the birds, one in relation to another, Mr Palomar feels caught in a weft whose continuity extends, uniform and without rents, as if he, too, were part of this moving body composed of hundreds and hundreds of bodies, detached, but forming a single object like a cloud or a column of smoke or a jet of water – something in other words, that even in the fluidity of its substance achieves a formal solidity of its own. But he only has to start following a single bird with his gaze and the disassociation of the elements returns; and the current he felt sustaining him, dissolve; the effect is that of a vertigo that grips him at the pit of the stomach.

This happens, for example, when Mr Palomar, after having convinced himself that the flock as a whole is flying towards his gaze to a bird that is, on the contrary, moving away, and from this one to another, also moving away... and he soon notices that all the birds that seemed to him to be approaching are in reality flying off in all directions as if he were in the centre of an explosion. But if he simply turns his eyes toward another zone of the sky there they are, concentrated over there, in an increasingly thick and crammed vortex, as, when a magnet hidden under a sheet of paper attracts iron filings, making patterns that become darker one moment, lighter the next, and in the end dissolve and leave on the white page a speckling of scattered fragments.

Hummingbird

Simon Schama (b. 1945)[38]

Last September, as the leaves in the Hudson valley began to colour, a ruby-throated hummingbird died in our living room. Its wings that beat 80 times a second; its heart that beat a thousand times a minute when hovering for nectar, were now still.

I touched them in self-reproach. Some months earlier a humming bird had got into the tall room through an opened window where the modernist curtain-glass wall overlooking our sloping back yard had made it lose its bearings. Rebounding from the false exit presented by the view through the glass I saw it fly frantically into a large abstract triptych hanging on another wall, over and over before finally escaping through a window I had opened some twenty feet up. Smoothing the dead bird's wings, I wondered if this time (perhaps the very same bird) had beat its last against the paintings. Had art, in league with modernist architectural asperity, killed it?

FROM

The Ancient Mariner
Samuel Taylor Coleridge (1772–1834)[39]

The ice was here, the ice was there
The ice was all around:
It cracked and growled, and roared and howled,
Like noises in a swound!

At length did cross an Albatross,
Thorough the fog it came;
As if it had been a Christian soul,
We hailed it in God's name.

It ate the food it ne'er had eat,
And round and round it flew.
The ice did split with a thunder-fit;
The helmsman steered us through!

And a good south wind sprung up behind;
The Albatross did follow,
And every day, for food or play,
Came to the mariner's hollo!

In mist or cloud, on mast or shroud,
It perched for vespers nine;
Whiles all the night, through fog-smoke white,
Glimmered the white Moon-shine.'

'God save thee, ancient Mariner!
From the fiends, that plague thee thus! –
Why look'st thou so?'
With my cross-bow
I shot the ALBATROSS.

FROM

The Birds
Daphne du Maurier (1907–1989)[40]

On December the third, the wind changed overnight, and it was winter. Until then the autumn had been mellow, soft. The leaves had lingered on the trees, golden-red, and the hedgerows were still green. The earth was rich where the plow had turned it.

Nat Hocken, because of a wartime disability, had a pension and did not work full time at the farm. He worked three days a week, and they gave him the lighter jobs: hedging, thatching, repairs to the farm buildings. Although he was married, with children, his was a solitary disposition; he liked best to work alone. It pleased him when he was given a bank to build up or a gate to mend at the far end of the peninsula, where the sea surrounded the farmland on either side. Then, at midday, he would pause and eat the pasty that his wife had baked for him and, sitting on the cliff's edge, would watch the birds. Autumn was best for this, better than spring. In spring the birds flew inland, purposeful, intent; they knew where they were bound; the rhythm and ritual of their life brooked no delay. In autumn those that had not migrated overseas but remained to pass the winter were caught up in the same driving urge, but because migration was denied them, followed a pattern of their own. Great flocks of them came to the peninsula, restless, uneasy, spending themselves in motion; now wheeling, circling in the sky, now settling to feed on the rich, new-turned soil; but even when they fed, it was as though they did so without hunger, without desire. Restlessness drove them to the skies again.

Black and white, jackdaw and gull, mingled in strange partnership, seeking some sort of liberation, never satisfied, never still. Flocks of starlings, rustling like silk, flew to fresh pasture, driven by the same necessity of movement, and the smaller birds, the finches and the larks, scattered from tree to hedge as if compelled.

Nat watched them, and he watched the sea birds too. Down in the bay they waited for the tide. They had more patience. Oystercatchers, redshank, sanderling, and curlew watched by the water's edge; as the slow sea sucked at the shore and then withdrew, leaving the strip of seaweed bare and the shingle churned, the sea birds raced and ran upon the beaches. Then that same impulse to flight seized upon them too. Crying, whistling, calling, they skimmed the placid sea and left the shore. Make haste, make speed, hurry and begone; yet where, and to what purpose? The restless urge of autumn, unsatisfying, sad, had put a spell upon them, and they must flock, and wheel, and cry; they must spill themselves of motion before winter came.

'Perhaps,' thought Nat, munching his pasty by the cliff's edge, 'a message comes to the birds in autumn, like a warning. Winter is coming. Many of them perish. And like people who, apprehensive of death before their time, drive themselves to work or folly, the birds do likewise.'

The birds had been more restless than ever this fall of the year, the agitation more marked because the days were still. As the tractor traced its path up and down the western hills, the figure of the farmer silhouetted on the driving seat, the whole machine and the man upon it, would be lost momentarily in the great cloud of wheeling, crying birds. There were many more than usual; Nat was sure of this. Always, in autumn, they followed the plow, but not in great flocks like these, nor with such clamor.

Nat remarked upon it when hedging was finished for the day. 'Yes,' said the farmer, 'there are more birds about than usual; I've noticed it too. And daring, some of them, taking no notice of the tractor. One or two gulls came so close to my head this afternoon I thought they'd knock my cap off! As it was, I could scarcely see what I was doing when they were overhead and I had the sun in my eyes. I have a notion the weather will change. It will be a hard winter. That's why the birds are restless.'... Not a sparrow chattered in the hedge beyond the garden gate, no early missel thrush or blackbird pecked on the grass for worms. There was no sound at all but the east wind and the sea.

Nat shut the window and the door of the small bedroom and went back across the passage to his own. His wife sat up in bed, one child asleep beside her, the smaller in her arms, his face bandaged. The curtains were tightly drawn across the window, the candles lit. Her face looked garish in the yellow light. She shook her head for silence.

'He's sleeping now,' she whispered, 'but only just. Something must have cut him, there was blood at the corner of his eyes. Jill said it was the birds. She said she woke up, and the birds were in the room.'

His wife looked up at Nat, searching his face for confirmation. She looked terrified, bewildered, and he did not want her to know that he was also shaken, dazed almost, by the events of the past few hours.

'There are birds in there,' he said, 'dead birds, nearly fifty of them. Robins, wrens, all the little birds from hereabouts. It's as though a madness seized them, with the east wind.' He sat down on the bed beside his wife and held her hand. 'It's the weather,' he said; 'it must be that, it's the hard weather. They aren't the birds, maybe, from here around. They've been driven down from upcountry.'

'But, Nat,' whispered his wife, 'it's only this night that the weather turned. There's been no snow to drive them. And they can't be hungry yet. There's food for them out there in the fields.' 'It's the weather,' repeated Nat. 'I tell you, it's the weather.'

'Bird'
Pablo Neruda (1904–1973)[41]

It was passed from one bird to another,
the whole gift of the day.
The day went from flute to flute,
went dressed in vegetation,
in flights which opened a tunnel
through the wind would pass
to where birds were breaking open
the dense blue air –
and there, night came in.

When I returned from so many journeys,
I stayed suspended and green
between sun and geography –
I saw how wings worked,
how perfumes are transmitted
by feathery telegraph,
and from above I saw the path,
the springs and the roof tiles,
the fishermen at their trades,
the trousers of the foam;
I saw it all from my green sky.
I had no more alphabet
than the swallows in their courses,
the tiny, shining water
of the small bird on fire
which dances out of the pollen.

FROM

Silent Spring
Rachel Carson (1907–1964)[42]

There was once a town in the heart of America where all life seemed to live in harmony with its surroundings. The town lay in the midst of a checkerboard of prosperous farms, with fields of grain and hillsides of orchards where, in spring, white clouds of bloom drifted above the green fields. In autumn, oak and maple and birch set up a blaze of color that flamed and flickered across a backdrop of pines.... The countryside was, in fact, famous for the abundance and variety of its bird life, and when the flood of migrants was pouring through in spring and fall people traveled from great distances to observe them. Others came to fish the streams, which flowed clear and cold out of the hills and contained shady pools where trout lay. So it had been from the days many years ago when the first settlers raised their houses, sank their wells, and built their barns. Then a strange blight crept over the area and everything began to change. Some evil spell had settled on the community: mysterious maladies swept the flocks of chickens; the cattle and sheep sickened and died. Everywhere was a shadow of death. The farmers spoke of much illness among their families. In the town the doctors had become more and more puzzled by new kinds of sickness appearing among their patients. There had been several sudden and unexplained deaths, not only among adults but even among children, who would be stricken suddenly while at play and die within a few hours.

There was a strange stillness. The birds, for example—where had they gone? Many people spoke of them, puzzled and disturbed. The feeding stations in the backyards were deserted. The few birds seen anywhere were moribund; they trembled violently and could not fly. It was a spring without voices. On the mornings that had once throbbed with the dawn chorus of robins, catbirds, doves, jays, wrens, and scores of other bird voices there was now no sound; only silence lay over the fields and woods and marsh. On the farms the hens brooded, but no chicks hatched.... In the gutters under the eaves and between the shingles of the roofs, a white granular powder still showed a few patches; some weeks before it had fallen like snow upon the roofs and the lawns, the fields and streams. No witchcraft, no enemy action had silenced the rebirth of new life in this stricken world. The people had done it themselves... This town does not actually exist, but it might easily have a thousand counterparts in America or elsewhere in the world. I know of no community that has experienced all the misfortunes I describe. Yet every one of these disasters has actually happened somewhere, and many real communities have already suffered a substantial number of them. A grim specter has crept upon us almost unnoticed, and this imagined tragedy may easily become a stark reality we all shall know. What has already silenced the voices of spring in countless towns in America?

'Rockin' Robin'
Leon René (1902–1982)[43]

He rocks in the treetop all the day long
Hoppin' and a-boppin' and a-singin' his song
All the little birds down Jaybird Street
Love to hear the robin go tweet tweet tweet

Rockin' robin, tweet! Tweet! Tweet!
Rockin' robin, tweet! Tweet! Tweet!
Go rockin' robin
'Cause we're really gonna rock tonight

Every little swallow, every chick-a-dee
Every little bird in the tall oak tree
The wise old owl, the big black crow
Flappin' their wings, singin' go bird go!

Rockin' robin, tweet! Tweet! Tweet!
Rockin' robin, tweet! Tweet! Tweet!
Go rockin' robin
'Cause we're really gonna rock tonight

Pretty little raven at the bird bandstand
Taught him how to do the bop and it was grand
They started going steady and a-bless my soul
He out-bopped the buzzard and the oriole!

He rocks in the tree top all the day long
Hoppin' and a-boppin' and a-singin' his song
All the little birdies down Jaybird Street
Love to hear the robin go tweet tweet tweet!

Rockin' robin, tweet! Tweet! Tweet!
Rockin' robin, tweet! Tweet! Tweet!
Go rockin' robin
'Cause we're really gonna rock tonight

1 T.H. Johnson and T. Ward (eds.), *The Letters of Emily Dickinson* (Cambridge, MA: Belknap Press of Harvard University Press, 1958).

2 L. Cumming, *Thunderclap*, published by Chatto & Windus. Copyright © Laura Cumming, 2023. Reprinted by permission of The Random House Group Limited.

3 https://russianlegacy.com/poetry-pushkin-little-bird?srsltid=AfmBOooClk_xMn6k-JbIya6Cf1NfO5EtoLBl6TBwshDS-Ki88K-JDgb7o.

4 https://www.lovingchinese.com/yang-wan-li-cold-sparrows-with-english-translations/.

5 H. Macdonald, *H Is For Hawk* (London: Vintage Books, 2015).

6 T. Hughes, *Lupercal* (London: Faber and Faber, 1960).

7 https://www.goodreads.com/quotes/54701-i-am-a-cage-in-search-of-a-bird.

8 *These Branching Moments: Forty Odes by Rumi*, trans. J. Moyne and C. Barks (Berkeley: Copper Beech Press, 1987).

9 https://tangshi.tuxfamily.org/baijuyi/0016.html.

10 http://wpwt.soton.ac.uk/trans/owl/owltrans.htm.

11 https://www.literature.com/book/the_raven_and_the_fox_2464.

12 https://allpoetry.com/The-Tame-Bird-Was-In-A-Cage.

13 C. Okigbo, *Labyrinths with Path of Thunder* (London: Heinemann, 1971).

14 Translation by P. Lennon of M. Slory, *Alsof men alles loslaat*, trans. M. van Kempen and E. Hart (Haarlem, 2018).

15 https://www.azlyrics.com/lyrics/bobmarley/threelittlebirds.html.

16 D.H. Reiman et al. (eds.), *The Complete Poetry of Percy Bysshe Shelley* (Baltimore: Johns Hopkins University Press, 2012).

17 R.W. Franklin (ed.), *The Poems of Emily Dickinson: Reading Edition* (Cambridge, MA: Belknap Press, 1999).

18 *The Diwan of Abu Fadl 'Abbas ibn al Ahnaf*, trans. A. Wormhoudt (Oskaloosa, IA: William Penn College, 1980).

19 https://www.washingtonpost.com/news/inspired-life/wp/2017/06/05/getting-back-to-a-place-where-birds-fly-around-uncooked/.

20 https://www.goodreads.com/quotes/7161941-i-once-asked-a-bird-how-is-it-that-you.

21 https://www.thebeatles.com/blackbird.

22 J.N. Serio and C. Beyers (eds.), *The Collected Poems of Wallace Stevens* (New York: Alfred A. Knopf, 2015).

23 http://www.ricorso.net/tx/Lectures/3-Authors/Lectures/JAJoyce/Materials/Ulysses/short/Ulysses_12-18.htm.

24 https://matsuobashohaiku.home.blog/category/birds-of-prey/.

25 https://www.poetryfoundation.org/poems/48042/brancusis-golden-bird.

26 https://archive.org/stream/TheEpicof-Gilgamesh_201606/eog_djvu.txt.

27 *The Bible: The New Cambridge Paragraph Edition. King James Version* (Cambridge: Cambridge University Press, 2005).

28 *The Arabian Nights Entertainments* (Chicago: Rand McNally & Company, 1914).

29 Translation by P. Lennon of *Een karavaan uit Perzië. Klassieke Perzische poëzie*, trans. J.T.P. de Bruijn (Amsterdam: Stichting Uitgeverij Bulaaq, 2016).

30 https://www.poetryfoundation.org/poems/48860/the-raven.

31 http://rudy.negenborn.net/catullus/text2/e2.htm, trans. J. Fortaperus.

32 J. Cats and R. Farlie, *Moral Emblems*, trans. R. Pigot (New York: D. Appleton & Co, 1860).

33 Translation by P. Lennon of *Een Arabische tuin - klassieke Arabische poezie*, trans. G.J. van Gelder (Amsterdam: Stichting Uitgeverij Bulaaq, 2008).

34 https://www.wisesayings.com/peacock-quotes/.

35 https://sites.dartmouth.edu/vsfd18/ovids-icarus/, trans. A.S. Kline.

36 J.M. Barrie, *Peter Pan and Wendy* (London/Sydney/Auckland/Toronto: Hodder and Stoughton, 1979).

37 I. Calvino, *Mr. Palomar*, trans. W. Weaver (Boston: Mariner Books, 1983).

38 Original written especially for this anthology.

39 S.T. Coleridge, *The Rime of the Ancient Mariner* (New York: The Collector's Library, 2017).

40 D. Du Maurie, *The Birds* (London: Virago Press, 2015).

41 P. Neruda, *Fully Empowered*, translated by A. Reid. Translation copyright © 1975 by A. Reid. Reprinted by permission of Farrar, Straus and Giroux. All rights reserved.

42 R. Carson, *Silent Spring* (Boston: Mariner Books, 2002).

43 https://www.allmusicals.com/lyrics/mjthemusical/rockinrobin.htm.

Why *BIRDS*?

Boussauw 2024
J. Boussauw, *Vogels in de cultuur*, Gorredijk 2024.

Oh, for the Wings...

Alberth 2010
S. Alberth, *Leonora Carrington: Surrealism, Alchemy and* Art, New York 2010.

Lewis 1957
D. Lewis, *Constantin Brancusi*, London 1957.

Rowell 1999
M. Rowell, *Brancusi vs The United States. The Historic Trial. 1928*, New York 1999.

Spear 1969
A.T. Spear, *Brancusi's Birds*, New York 1969.

Spurling 1954
H. Spurling, *Matisse the Master. The Conquest of Colour 1909–1954*, London 1954.

Stone-Ferrier 2016
L. Stone-Ferrier, 'The Engagement of Carel Fabritius's Goldfinch of 1654 with the Dutch Window, a Significant Site of Neighborhood Social Exchange,' *Journal of Historians of Netherlandish Art* 8 (2016), no. 1, DOI: 10.5092/jhna.2016.8.1.5, http://www.jhna.org/index.php/vol-8-1-2016/325-stone-ferrier.

Utley 2000
G.R. Utley, *Pablo Picasso: The Communist Years*, New Haven 2000.

Who Doesn't Want to be Friends with *The Goldfinch*?

Bierens de Haan 1933
J.A. Bierens de Haan, 'Der Stieglitz als Schöpfer', *Journal fur Ornithologie* 81 (1933), pp. 1–22.

Boström 1950
K. Boström, 'De oorspronkelijke bestemming van C. Fabritius' Puttertje', *Oud Holland* 65 (1950), pp. 81–83.

Broos 1987
B. Broos, *Meesterwerken in het Mauritshuis*, The Hague 1987.

Brown 1981
C. Brown, *Carel Fabritius*, Oxford 1981.

Cats 1712
J. Cats, *Alle de wercken*, vol. 1, Amsterdam 1712.

Chomel 1743
M.N. Chomel, *Huishoudelyk woordboek*, Leiden/Amsterdam 1743.

Cumming 2023
L. Cumming, *Thunderclap: A Memoir of Art and Life and Sudden Death*, London 2023.

Van Deursen 2009
Chr. van Deursen, 'Tussen trekbank en roerlijn: Geschiedenis van de vinkenbanen in de duinstreek', in *Fitis* 45 (2009), no. 3, pp. 124–130.

Friedmann 1946
H. Friedmann, *The Symbolic Goldfinch: Its History and Significance in European Devotional Art*, Washington 1946.

The Hague/Schwerin 2004–2005a
F. Duparc, 'Carel Fabritius (1622–1654). Zijn leven en zijn werk', in F. Duparc et al., *Carel Fabritius 1622–1654*, exh. cat., The Hague (Mauritshuis), Schwerin (Staatliches Museum) 2004–2005.

The Hague/Schwerin 2004–2005b
A. van Suchtelen, 'Het Puttertje', in F. Duparc et al., *Carel Fabritius 1622–1654*, exh. cat., The Hague (Mauritshuis), Schwerin (Staatliches Museum) 2004–2005.

De Jongh 1967
E. de Jongh, *Zinne- en minnebeelden in de schilderkunst van de zeventiende eeuw*, Amsterdam 1967.

Van der Mark 2004
B. van der Mark, 'De Delftsche Donderslagh', *Mauritshuis in focus* 17 (2004), pp. 20-22.

Martin 1906
H. Martin, *Les miniaturistes français*, Paris 1906.

Matthey 2002
I. Matthey, *Vincken moeten vincken locken. Vijf eeuwen vangst van zangvogels en kwartels in Holland*, Hilversum 2002.

Moser 2023
B. Moser, *The Upside-Down World: Meeting with the Dutch Masters*, London 2023.

New York 2013
Vermeer, Rembrandt, and Hals: Masterpieces of Dutch Painting from the Mauritshuis, exh. cat., New York (The Frick Collection) 2013.

Noble et al. 2008
P. Noble et al., 'Het puttertje', in P. Noble, S. Meloni & C. Pottasch (eds.), *Bewaard voor de eeuwigheid*, The Hague/Zwolle 2008, pp. 146–155.

Schatborn 2006
P. Schatborn, 'Drawings attributed to Carel Fabritius', *Oud Holland* 119 (2006), pp. 130–138.

Seelig 2006
G. Seelig, 'The Dating of Fabritius's Stay in Amsterdam', *Oud Holland* 119 (2006), pp. 93–98.

Steendam 1649–1651
J. Steendam, *Den distelvink*, Amsterdam 1649–1651.

Stone-Ferrier 2016
L. Stone-Ferrier, 'The Engagement of Carel Fabritius's Goldfinch of 1654 with the Dutch Window, a Significant Site of Neighborhood Social Exchange', *Journal of Historians of Netherlandish Art* 8 (2016), no. 1, pp. 1–32.

Suzman Jowell 2016
F. Suzman Jowell, 'The Goldfinch's Travels. Fact and fiction', in B. Cornelis et al. (eds.), *Collecting for the Public. Works that Made a Difference: Essays for Peter Hecht*, The Hague/London/Paris 2016, pp. 72–77.

Tartt 2013
D. Tartt, *The Goldfinch*, London 2013.

Thóth-Ubbens 1969
M. Thóth-Ubbens, 'Kijken naar het vogeltje', in *Miscellanea I.Q. van Regteren Altena: 16/V/1969*, Amsterdam 1969, pp. 233–240.

Vienna 2025
L. Van Sloten, 'Rembrandt and Samuel van Hoogstraten and their Passion for Illusions', in S. Pénot et al., *Rembrandt Hoogstraten: Colour and Illusion*, exh. cat., Vienna (Kunsthistorisches Museum) 2025.

Wadum 2004
J. Wadum, 'Het puttertje gerestaureerd en doorgelicht', *Mauritshuis in focus* 17 (2004), no. 2, pp. 24–30.

Zwagerman 2015
J. Zwagerman, 'Het Puttertje. Carel Fabritius en Donna Tartt', in J. Zwagerman, *De stilte van het licht. Schoonheid en onbehagen in de kunst*, Amsterdam 2015, pp. 103–109.

Stilled Flight

Boethius 2009
Anicius Manlius Severinus Boethius, *The Consolation of Philosophy*, W.V. Cooper (trans.), 2009, http://www.exclassics.com/consol/consol.pdf. Accessed on 13 September 2025.

Boussauw 2024
J. Boussauw, *Vogels in de cultuur*, Gorredijk 2024.

Idema 2025
W.I. Idema, *A Historical Taxonomy of Talking Birds in Chinese Literature*, Cambridge 2025.

Van der Jagt 2022
I. van der Jagt, 'De valkerij en het veranderende beeld van de vrouw', in J.L. van Zanden (ed.), *Gevleugelde geschiedenis van Nederland. De Nederlanders en hun vogels*, Amsterdam 2022.

De Jongh 1967
E. de Jongh, 'Erotica in vogelperspectief. De dubbelzinnigheid van een reeks zeventiende-eeuwse genrevoorstellingen', *Nederlands Kunsthistorisch Jaarboek* 18 (1967), pp. 115–146.

Lambrecht 2022
T. Lambrecht, 'De zwarte gesel van de boer', in J.L. van Zanden (ed.), *Gevleugelde geschiedenis van Nederland. De Nederlanders en hun vogels*, Amsterdam 2022.

Martens 2010
J. Martens, 'De Valkerij', *Geschiedenis.nl*, 30 May 2010, https://geschiedenis.nl/nieuws/artikel/3195/de-valkerij. Accessed on 13 September 2025.

***Natuurhistorisch Museum Rotterdam* n.d.**
'Kluifrègâh bijgezet in expo "Dode dieren met een verhaal"', *Natuurhistorisch Museum Rotterdam*, https://www.hetnatuurhistorisch.nl/nieuws/kluifregah-bijgezet-in-expo-dode-dieren-met-een-verhaal. Accessed on 13 September 2025.

Temmerman 2020
T. Temmerman, *'Alte Schoone Ende Vremde Dieren': De blik op dieren in Bourgondische reisverslagen (15de eeuw). Dieren in de reisverslagen van Guillebert de Lannoy, Bertrandon de la Broquière, Jan Adornes, en Joos van Ghistele*, Master's thesis, University of Ghent, 2020, https://libstore.ugent.be/fulltxt/RUG01/002/862/696/RUG01-002862696_2020_0001_AC.pdf. Accessed on 13 September 2025.

***Wikipedia* n.d.**
'Grey heron', *Wikipedia*, https://en.wikipedia.org/wiki/Grey_heron. Accessed on 14 September 2025.

The Fate of the Flightless

***Beter leven. Dierenbescherming* n.d.**
'Leghennen', *Beter leven. Dierenbescherming*, https://beterleven.dierenbescherming.nl/over-de-dieren/alle-dieren/leghennen/. Accessed on 9 September 2025.

Van der Gulden 2014
P. van der Gulden, 'Kip scharrelt al lang op het erf van de mens', *de Volkskrant*, 25 November 2014, https://www.volkskrant.nl/wetenschap/kip-scharrelt-al-lang-op-het-erf-van-de-mens~ba429edb/. Accessed on 10 September 2025.

***Immaterieel Erfgoed* n.d.**
'"Tsougkrisma"! Rode eieren tikken op Grieks-orthodox Pasen', *Immaterieel Erfgoed*, https://immaterieelerfgoed.be/nl/erfgoederen/tsougkrisma-rode-eieren-tikken-op-grieks-orthodox-pasen. Accessed on 9 September 2025.

***Nederland in cijfers* n.d.**
'Hoeveel landbouwdieren telt ons land?', *Nederland in cijfers*, https://longreads.cbs.nl/nederland-in-cijfers-2021/hoeveel-landbouwdieren-telt-ons-land. Accessed on 9 September 2025.

***Wakker dier* 2023**
'Start juridische procedure: kippen te weinig leefruimte', *Wakker dier*, https://www.wakkerdier.nl/persberichten/juridische-procedure-kippen-te-weinig-leefruimte/. Accessed on 9 September 2025.

***World Animal Protection* 2018**
''s Werelds meest gegeten vlees', *World Animal Protection*, https://www.worldanimalprotection.nl/nieuws/s-werelds-meest-gegeten-vlees/#. Accessed on 9 September 2025.

Plumage

***BBC News* 2015**
'Almost 300 years without a duvet', *BBC News*, https://www.bbc.com/news/magazine-34848546. Accessed on 11 September 2025.

Mantingh 2022
E. Mantingh, 'Ik probeer mijn ganzenveer: over vogels die geschiedenis schreven', in J.L. van Zanden et al., *Gevleugelde geschiedenis van Nederland. De Nederlanders en hun vogels*, Amsterdam 2022.

Van Mensch 1978
P.J.A. van Mensch, 'Archeologie en vogels', *Het Vogeljaar* 26 (1978), no. 5, pp. 219–223, https://natuurtijdschriften.nl/pub/543078/HVJ1978026005004.pdf. Accessed on 10 September 2025.

***VRT NWS* 2024**
'Veer van uitgestorven huia-vogel geveild voor meer dan 26.000 euro in Nieuw-Zeeland', *VRT NWS*, https://www.vrt.be/vrtnws/nl/2024/05/22/duurste-veer-ooit-geveild-in-nieuw-zeeland/. Accessed on 11 September 2025.

Envying Avians

Kane 2002
D.D. Kane, 'Science in the Art of the Italian Renaissance II: Leonardo Da Vinci's Representation of Animals in His Works', *Ohio Journal of Science* 102 (2002), no. 5, pp. 113–115, https://kb.osu.edu/server/api/core/bitstreams/d2fbf50c-13ab-521e-a70c-710d8a6ef1bb/content. Accessed on 24 August 2025.

***National Air and Space Museum/ Smithsonian* 2013**
'Leonardo da Vinci and Flight', *National Air and Space Museum/Smithsonian,* https://airandspace.si.edu/stories/editorial/leonardo-da-vinci-and-flight. Accessed on 3 September 2025.

Schleif 2010
C. Schleif, 'Albrecht Dürer between Agnes Frey and Willibald Pirckheimer', in L. Silver and J.C. Smith (eds.) *The Essential Dürer*, Philadelphia 2010, pp. 185–208.

Toliver 2018
Z. Toliver, "Is Leonardo da Vinci the Forefather of the Animal Rights Movement?", *PETA*, 12 April 2018, https://www.peta.org/news/leonardo-da-vinci-animal-rights-pioneer/. Accessed on 24 August 2025.

The Genius of Birds

Birkhead 2008
T. Birkhead, *De wijsheid van vogels. Een geïllustreerde geschiedenis van de ornithologie*, Amsterdam 2008.

Hiemstra et al. 2023
A.F. Hiemstra et al.,'Bird nests made from anti-bird spikes', *Deinsea* 21 (2023), pp. 17–25.

***Vogelbescherming Nederland* 2023**
'Waarom zwermende spreeuwen nooit botsen', *Vogelbescherming Nederland,* https://www.vogelbescherming.nl/actueel/bericht/waarom-zwermende-spreeuwen-nooit-botsen?. Accessed on 25 August 2025.

Heavenly Messengers

***The Art Newspaper* n.d.**
'National Museum of Denmark returns sacred Indigenous cloack to Brazil', *The Art Newspaper,* https://www.theartnewspaper.com/2024/09/17/national-museum-denmark-returns-sacred-indigenous-cloak-brazil. Accessed on 19 September 2025.

***Beleven* n.d.**
'De vogel Milcham', *Beleven,* https://www.beleven.org/verhaal/de_vogel_milcham#. Accessed on 19 September 2025.

Hulspas 2015
M. Hulspas, *De vliegende koningin van Sheba (en haar zwempoging)*, 2015, https://marcelhulspas.nl/home/de-vliegende-koningin-van-sheba-en-haar. Accessed on 19 September 2025.

***The Guardian* 2024**
'"Our culture is dying": vulture shortage threatens Zoroastrian burial rites', *The Guardian,* https://www.theguardian.com/world/article/2024/may/04/vulture-shortage-threatens-zoroastrian-burial-rites-india-iran-pakistan. Accessed on 28 September 2025.

Van Maerlant 1995
J. van Maerlant, *Het boek der natuur,* Peter Burger (ed.), Amsterdam 1995, https://www.dbnl.org/tekst/maer002dern03_01/maer002dern03_01_0004.php. Accessed on 19 September 2025.

***Mauritshuis* n.d.**
'Diara Tukano', *Mauritshuis,* https://www.mauritshuis.nl/en/what-s-on/museum-murals/daiara-tukano. Accessed on 19 September 2025.

Mulders 2021
H. Mulders, *De ontdekking van de natuur,* Amsterdam 2021.

***My articles* 2022**
'The Conference of the Birds', *My articles,* https://myarticles.io/the-conference-of-the-birds/. Accessed on 19 September 2025.

Riclefs 2022
N. Riclefs, 'How Angels Found their Wings', *History Today* 72 (2022), no. 12, https://www.historytoday.com/archive/history-matters/how-angels-found-their-wings. Accessed on 28 September 2025.

Verduin n.d.
K. Verduin, 'Nieuws uit Afrika', https://web.universiteitleiden.nl/fsw/verduin/sofa/sofa_fen.htm. Accessed on 19 September 2025.

Lovebirds

Boussauw 2024
J. Boussauw, *Vogels in de cultuur,* Gorredijk 2024.

Cole 2010
I. Cole, 'Pablo Picasso: The Development of a Peace Symbol', *Art Times* (May/June 2010), https://www.arttimesjournal.com/art/reviews/May_June_10_Ina_Cole/Pablo_Picasso_Ina_Cole.html. Accessed on 31 August 2025.

Dalzell and Victor 2015
T. Dalzell and T. Victor (eds.), *The New Partridge Dictionary of Slang and Unconventional English,* London/New York 2015.

Ferriss and Young 2006
S. Ferriss and M. Young, 'Chicks, Girls and Choice: Redefining Feminism', *Junctures* 6 (2006), pp. 87–97, https://www.junctures.org/index.php/junctures/article/view/121. Accessed on 30 August 2025.

***Tate* n.d.**
'Dove, 1949, Pablo Picasso', *Tate,* https://www.tate.org.uk/art/artworks/picasso-dove-p11366. Accessed on 31 August 2025.

***Wikipedia* n.d.**
'Cock', *Wikipedia,* https://en.wikipedia.org/wiki/Cock_(slang). Accessed on 30 August 2025.

Photo Credits

Albertina Art Museum Wien, Vienna: p. 106, 170.

Archives Charmet / Bridgeman Images: p. 127 (top).

Art Institute of Chicago/Art Resource, NY/ Scala, Florence - SABAM Belgium 2026: p. 21 (top right).

Biblioteca Vaticana, Vatican City, Pal. lat 1071: p. 60.

BirdLife Netherlands: p. 93 (bottom).

Bodleian Libraries, University of Oxford, Oxford: p. 147.

Bpk/Kupferstichkabinett, SMB/Dietmar Katz: p. 107 (top).

Bridgeman Images: p. 48, 53 (bottom), 59, 125, 126 (bottom), 127 (bottom).

Bridgeman Images – Succession Brancusi – All rights reserved (SABAM) 2026: p. 18.

Clarence Buckingham Collection, The Art Institute of Chicago, Chicago: p. 165.

Collection Betty and Homero Aridjis: p. 36, 155.

Collection Kröller-Müller Museum, Otterlo, photo Cary Markerink: p. 76.

Collection Wereldmuseum Rotterdam: p. 102.

Dordrechts Museum, Dordrecht: p. 83.

Eet!verleden, photo Jeroen Savelkouls: pp. 80–81.

E. Meijer: 157 (middle and bottom), p. 158, 159 (bottom).

Fondation Henri Cartier-Bresson/ Magnum Photos: p. 28 (top), 140.

Foundation Peggy Guggenheim Collection, Venice – Succession Brancusi – All rights reserved (SABAM) 2026: p. 16 (bottom), 121.

Galleria degli Uffizi, Florence: p. 49 (right).

G.C. Heemskerk: p. 156, 157 (top), 159 (top).

Getty Images: p. 41 (left and middle), 77, 91 (top).

Greenpeace Netherlands, Amsterdam: p. 70.

Huis van het boek, The Hague: p. 128.

Image select/Alamy: p. 39 (bottom left), 146 (bottom).

Iris van Herpen, Amsterdam: p. 41 (right), 103.

Istock: p. 115.

Jan van IJken, Beesd: p. 43, 116–117.

KB – National Library of the Netherlands, The Hague: p. 126 (top).

Kenwood House, London: p. 24.

Kröller-Müller Museum, Otterlo, Succession H. Matisse – SABAM Belgium 2026: p. 32.

Kunstmuseum The Hague: p. 65.

Larousse pour tous: p. 88.

Library of Congress, Washington, DC: p. 93 (top), 171 (left).

Liechtenstein – The Princely Collections: p. 49 (left).

Louise Lawler: p. 154.

Mauritshuis, The Hague: p. 16 (top), 25, 44, 45, 68, 73, 78–79, 86, 89, 91(bottom), 95, 129, 131, 142, 145, 148, 149, 160, 166–167.

Mauritshuis, The Hague, photo Fred Ernst: p. 134.

Michel Sima – SABAM Belgium 2026/ Bridgeman Images: p. 30 (bottom right).

The Morgan Library, New York: p. 46.

Musée du Louvre, dist. GrandPalaisRmn/ Marc Jeanneteau: p. 92 (left).

Museo Nacional del Prado, Madrid: p. 31, 37.

Museo Nacional Thyssen-Bornemisza, Madrid: p. 172, 174.

Museum Arnhem, on long-term loan from the Collection of the Cultural Heritage Agency of the Netherlands, photo Marc Pluim: p. 53 (top).

Museum Boijmans Van Beuningen, Rotterdam, photo Studio Tromp: p. 20 (top), 52, 56, 72.

Museum Boijmans Van Beuningen, Rotterdam. From the estate of Dr. J.C.J. Bierens de Haan/photo Studio Tromp: p. 51.

Museum Catharijneconvent, Utrecht, photo Ruben de Heer: p. 122, 132–133.

The Museum of Modern Art, New York: p. 38 (top), 39 (top).

The Museum of Modern Art, New York/ Scala, Florence – SABAM Belgium 2026: p. 34 (left), 35, 40.

Museum Speelklok, Utrecht: p. 62, 63.

Museum Voorlinden, Wassenaar: pp. 108–109.

Napishtim: p. 124.

Natural History Museum, London/ Bridgeman Images: p. 171 (right).

Nationalmuseet, Copenhagen, photo Roberto Fortuna: p. 130.

Naturalis, Leiden: p. 120.

Natuurhistorisch Museum, Rotterdam: p. 66, 69.

NGF – Nikolaus Geyrhalter Filmproduktion GmbH, Vienna: p. 84.

Pat de Groot: p. 168.

Pont d'Arc caves, Chauvet: p. 15.

Rijksmuseum, Amsterdam: p. 20 (bottom), 39 (bottom right), 47, 64, 71, 74, 82, 94, 97, 98–99, 104, 111, 112, 119, 135, 144, 150–151.

Rijksmuseum Twenthe, Enschede: p. 50, 132.

Rijksmuseum van Oudheden, Leiden: p. 27, 136, 137, 138, 139.

Royal Collection Enterprises Limited [2026] | Royal Collection Trust: p. 110.

Royal Collection Trust/© His Majesty King Charles III, 2026/Bridgeman Images: p. 38 (bottom).

RX&SLAG, Paris/New York: p. 21 (bottom), 85.

Studio Tracey Emin, White Cube Gallery, London: p. 42 (bottom), 152–153.

Succession H. Matisse/Bridgeman Images: p. 28 (bottom).

Succession Picasso – SABAM Belgium 2026/Bridgeman: p. 29 (top), 33.

Succession Picasso – SABAM Belgium 2026/Picasso Museum, Barcelona: p. 30 (bottom left).

Succession Picasso – SABAM Belgium 2026/Picasso Museum, Münster: p. 30 (bottom), 141.

Teylers Museum, Haarlem – Succession Brancusi – All rights reserved (SABAM) 2026: p. 23, 67, 161, 162, 163.

The Trustees of the British Museum: p. 92 (right), 146 (top).

Veneranda Biblioteca Ambrosiana/ Mondadori Portfolio, Milan: p. 107 (bottom).

VG Bild-Kunst, photo Juliana Schönrock – SABAM Belgium 2026: p. 34 (right).

Wereldmuseum Amsterdam/Leiden: p. 90, 96, 100, 101.

Young & Rubicam Amsterdam (now VML), Koninklijke Luchtmacht Maatschappij (KLM), Amstelveen: p. 109.

Colophon

This catalogue was published to accompany the exhibition *BIRDS – Curated by The Goldfinch & Simon Schama* Mauritshuis, The Hague (12 February – 7 June 2026)

Authors
Laura Cumming
Martine Gosselink
Stefan Hertmans
Philip Hoare
Eva Meijer
Adrienne Quarles van Ufford
Simon Schama

Translation
Patrick Lennon (Dutch–English)

Anthology
Martine Gosselink
Simon Schama

Picture research
Julie Hartkamp (Mauritshuis)
Séverine Lacante (Hannibal Books)

Copy-editing
Cath Phillips

Project management
Suzan van den Berg (Mauritshuis)
Sara Colson (Hannibal Books)

Art director
Natacha Hofman

Design
Tim Bisschop

Production
Stichting Koninklijk Kabinet van Schilderijen Mauritshuis, The Hague

Retouching
Fotorama

Printing
Printer Trento, Italy

Publisher
Gautier Platteau

Mauritshuis

ISBN 978 94 9341 651 2
D/2026/11922/04
NUR 654

This catalogue has also been published in a Dutch edition:
ISBN 978 94 9341 652 9
D/2026/11922/05
NUR 654

Stichting Koninklijk Kabinet van Schilderijen Mauritshuis, Den Haag / The Hague
www.hannibalbooks.be
www.mauritshuis.nl

First edition: February 2026
Second edition: March 2026

Hannibal Books team
Laura Bijnens, Sara Colson, Pieter De Meyere, Natacha Hofman, Séverine Lacante, Sofie Meert, Gautier Platteau, Hedwig Scheltjens, Stephanie Van den Bosch, Hadewych Van den Bossche

Cover (front and back)
Carel Fabritius, *The Goldfinch*, 1654.
Oil on panel, 33.5 × 22.8 cm.
Mauritshuis, The Hague.

Thanks to

Major partners
Ministerie van Onderwijs, Cultuur en Wetenschap
VriendenLoterij

Exhibition partners
Stichting de Johan Maurits Compagnie
Stichting Vrienden van het Mauritshuis
Lucas Fonds
Fonds 'De Opzet'
Dutch Masters Foundation
Stichting Thurkowfonds

Lenders
His Majesty King Charles III, United Kingdom
Atelier Iris van Herpen, Amsterdam
Betty and Homero Aridjis, Mexico
Bodleian Library, Oxford
Dordrechts Museum, Dordrecht
Fondation Cartier-Bresson, Paris
Galerie RX&SLAG | Paris Le Marais, Paris
Greenpeace Nederland, Amsterdam
Jan van IJken Photography & Film, Beesd
KLM – Koninklijke Luchtvaart Maatschappij, Amstelveen
Kunstmuseum Pablo Picasso, Münster
Kunstmuseum The Hague
LeWitt Collection, Chester, CT (USA)
Manon Henzen, Eet!verleden, Nijmegen
Museum Boijmans Van Beuningen, Rotterdam
Museum Catharijneconvent, Utrecht
Museum Speelklok, Utrecht
Museum Voorlinden, Wassenaar
Natural History Museum, Rotterdam
Naturalis Biodiversity Center, Leiden
Nikolaus Geyrhalter Filmproduktion GmbH
Peggy Guggenheim Collection, Venice (Solomon R. Guggenheim Foundation, New York)
Rijksmuseum, Amsterdam
Rijksmuseum Twenthe, Enschede
Rijksmuseum van Oudheden, Leiden
Studio Tracey Emin, courtesy White Cube Gallery, London
Teylers Museum, Haarlem
Wereldmuseum Amsterdam, Leiden, Rotterdam